The New American Olive Oil

The New American Olive Oil

PROFILES OF ARTISAN PRODUCERS AND 75 RECIPES

FRAN GAGE

Photographs by Maren Caruso

Stewart, Tabori & Chang
New York

Published in 2009 by Stewart, Tabori & Chang
An imprint of Harry N. Abrams, Inc.

Library of Congress Cataloging-in-Publication Data

Gage, Fran.
  The new American olive oil : profiles of artisan producers and 75
recipes / by Fran Gage; photographs by Maren Caruso.
    p. cm.
  Includes bibliographical references and index.
  ISBN 978-1-58479-754-8
1. Cookery (Olive oil) 2. Olive oil. 3. Olive oil industry—United
States. I. Title.
  TX819.O42G34 2009
  641.6'463--dc22
                                    2008029536

Editor: Luisa Weiss
Designer: LeAnna Weller Smith
Production Manager: Tina Cameron

The text of this book was composed in Aaux Pro and Adobe Caslon.

Printed and bound in China
10 9 8 7 6 5 4 3 2 1

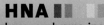

HNA
harry n. abrams, inc.
a subsidiary of La Martinière Groupe
115 West 18th Street
New York, NY 10011
www.hnabooks.com

FOR CASEY AND CLAIRE

CONTENTS

Introduction

I was a latecomer to extra-virgin olive oil. The fat of choice when I was growing up was margarine. My mother used it for cooking, and we spread it on toast for breakfast and on the rolls we occasionally ate at dinner. For special occasions and holidays, a dish of butter was on the table. I don't remember olive oil at all.

Shortly after my husband and I were married, we were smitten by the food we ate during a monthlong trip to France. We returned home, bought Julia Child's books, and started cooking. Butter became a major presence in our kitchen. We whisked it with abandon into sauces. Cooked vegetables were bathed in it. Sometimes we mixed it with a little flavorless oil and used it as a sauté medium. We made vinaigrette for salads with that same tasteless oil. Maybe we used olive oil sometimes, but if we did, I'm sure it was a dubious oil from a supermarket. Having little exposure to the real thing, I wouldn't have known the difference.

Then I became obsessed with French pastry. I went to France to learn more and eventually opened a bakery up the street from our house in San Francisco. We bought butter in sixty-pound blocks. Good pastry demands butter, and that's all we used. We did make *fougasse*, which contained olive oil, but it certainly wasn't extra-virgin and I know I wouldn't use that oil now.

Years later, I signed up for an Olive Oil Sensory Evaluation Course given by the University of California Extension Service as part of my research for a book project. I tasted more olive oil in two days than I had tasted in the previous six months. My taste buds were awakened, but although olive oil crept into our kitchen, butter still reigned supreme.

Five years passed. I received a letter. The California Olive Oil Council was looking for additional members for its taste panel.

Because of the sensory evaluation course I had taken, I was invited to take an arrangement test, a tool that assesses innate ability to detect subtle variations in olive oil defects. My score led to an offer to join the panel. I started tasting olive oil twice a month. Eventually I was also asked to join the University of California at Davis research panel that meets on weeks that alternate with the COOC schedule. Although we primarily taste California olive oil, those from other countries—including defective oils to keep us on our toes—are slipped into the sessions. My olive oil knowledge has increased a hundredfold. I've judged oils at the Los Angeles International Extra-Virgin Olive Oil Competition for the past three years.

I'm always on the lookout for bottles of extra-virgin olive oil that I haven't yet tasted, and I continue to marvel at the subtle differences that can occur in oil. Although my stash of extra-virgin olive oils—stored in wine cartons in a cool closet off the kitchen—might dwindle a little now that this book is complete, I know I will always have several of each style of extra-virgin olive oil (delicate, medium, and robust) as well as a selection of flavored olive oils available. They're the only oils I use now.

Once I tasted the good stuff, there was no going back.

All About Olive Oil

OLIVES INTO OIL

Making olive oil seems straightforward—crush olives and separate the oil from the pulp. Excessive heat and harsh chemicals, essential to the refining of seed oils, aren't needed. But careful attention to detail at each step in the process can make the difference between a great extra-virgin olive oil and a bad one. Many factors and decisions influence the outcome of an olive's journey from a tree to your kitchen—the variety of tree, the farming practices, the timing of the harvest, the milling and storage, the blending, the bottling, and the display in a retail store.

California olive orchards are a mix of old trees from the days of the missions to twelve-inch transplants of hybrid varieties, and everything in between. Some of the old olive trees are tall, making harvest difficult; by contrast, the newer semidwarf trees are harvested by lumbering machines that strip them of fruit quickly. The number of olive trees on each acre of orchard land varies from 120 to 670. Most new plantings of standard-size olive trees require patience—it may take five or seven years to get a crop. Olive trees live, on average, three hundred to six hundred years, although there are reports of a tree in Portugal that is two thousand years old, and another in Greece that has lived for six thousand years. Although these gnarled, thousand-year-old trees in poor soil without water will produce olives, the modern orchardist knows that better soil, irrigation, careful pruning, and pest management increase the odds of a successful harvest. If the trees are well tended and the weather cooperates, a grower may get four tons of olives per acre and can produce about forty gallons of oil per ton.

There are thousands of olive varieties, but only 150 account for more than 90 percent of the world's production. Thirty varieties are grown commercially in California, although some producers have small stands of more unusual olives that they blend into their oils. Although all olives share the same botanical name, *Olea europaea*, the trees have distinctions. Some are self-fertile; others need a nearby tree of a different variety to produce fruit. Some are cold-hardy; others not. Some bear fruit earlier than others. Some of the fruit is small; some is the size of plums. And some varietals yield more oil per pound than others.

The most important factor affecting the taste of an extra-virgin olive oil is the variety of olive. For example, Arbequina, Leccino, and Maurino olives produce more delicate oils, while Frantoio, Koroneiki, and Moraiolo oils, with their higher polyphenol levels, are robust. Two other important factors influence the taste—the maturity of the olives at harvest and their handling and processing.

In California, olives are harvested from October until February. The fruit on any tree doesn't ripen at the same time, so the grower looks at the fruit, testing the olives for maturity using a system developed by the International Olive Oil Council in 1984, waiting until there is a mix of green and riper fruit. Greener fruit will produce more bitterness; darker fruit yields more oil, and that oil will be more delicate. Ideally, the trees are harvested when there is a mix of both.

There are various ways to dislodge the olives from the trees. Hand harvesting is preferred by many, but this is extraordinarily costly; it can account for up to 65 percent of production costs. Workers wearing gloves strip the olives from the branches into picking bags, then transfer them into orchard baskets. Taller olive trees require ladders, increasing the risk of injury. Hand-held pneumatic combs and rotary pickers with extension poles make the task a little more efficient.

Another option is a trunk shaker. A machine with claw-like protrusions grips a tree and shakes the olives onto a waiting tarpaulin on the ground or into an unfolding umbrella attached to the machine.

Over-the-row machine harvesters are very efficient for super-high-density orchards, a recent innovation in which the trees are spaced very close together.

While on the tree, the olives are in perfect condition, but as soon as they are picked, enzymes start to degrade the fruit, so they must be handled with care. Olives stored in piles will heat up and start to ferment. Wet olives may mold. Orchard bins should be ventilated and be shallow enough that the fruit isn't crushed. Most important, the olives should be milled as soon as possible after picking. Twenty-four hours is the outer window for processing.

Upon arrival at the mill, the olives go through a blower (to remove leaves) and then a washer. Next the olives are crushed to break the cells so the oil can be extracted. For centuries olives were crushed with heavy stones, often turned by animals. Stone mills have been part of the lore of the olive as long as people have been making olive oil. But in today's world they are disappearing, especially in California. They are bulky, slow, and discontinuous. Because stone mills are slower and more open than other methods, the olive paste is subjected to more oxygen, increasing the risk of degradation. Paradoxically, this exposure, which decreases the antioxidant properties of very bitter olives and thus tames the taste, is sometimes desirable.

Hammer mills have largely replaced stones. They are small machines, considering the work they do. Blades inside a metal casing rotate at high speed, crushing the olives and forcing them through a metal screen. As one miller told me, "The stone is gentle, the hammer violent." Because the hammer mill pulverizes the fruit, the olive oil and solids emulsify more, requiring longer mixing in the next phase.

A disc mill produces an olive paste with a consistency between those made by a stone and a hammer. It slices the fruit rather than smashing it.

Another variation is the pitter mill, which removes the pits of the olives. Few of these are in use. Most millers think that fruitiness, bitterness, and pungency, characteristics of good olive oil, suffer when the pits are removed.

In a traditional operation, after the olives had been reduced to a paste by stones, the olive oil makers spread the paste on mats, stacked them, then exerted pressure using a screw or, later, a hydraulic press to force the oil from the solids. This method often caused oxidation of the olive oil, and because it was difficult to clean the mats, later batches of oil could be contaminated.

Instead of mats, modern millers put the paste into a jacketed vessel called a malaxation tank, where spiral paddles slowly mix it, encouraging the oil droplets to separate from the solids and coalesce. Water surrounding the tank is heated to encourage separation, but just barely: between 77 and 86 degrees Fahrenheit. Higher temperatures can mar the flavor.

When the miller deems that the olive paste is ready, it is pumped from the malaxation tank into a horizontal centrifugal decanter that separates the oil by spinning at about three thousand revolutions per minute. There are two types of centrifugal decanters, three-phase and two-phase, so called because of the end products that result from processing. Water is added to the three-phase system, and the output is dry solids, fruit water, and olive oil. Problems in disposing of the fruit water and a demand for higher-quality olive oil led to the development of the two-phase system in 1992. The two-phase machine doesn't need additional water and produces olive oil and fruit water mixed with solids. Many millers strongly favor the two-phase system because the olive oil's polyphenols are not washed away.

The Sinolea, or selective filtration, system is an alternative to the horizontal centrifuge for separating oil from the olive paste. The paste passes from the malaxation tank to the Sinolea. Seven thousand stainless-steel blades dip into the paste; only the oil clings to them and it is wiped off the blades by rubber nubs. It is complicated equipment, and only one is in operation in California.

Some water and solid particles still remain in the olive oil after it leaves the horizontal centrifuge or the Sinolea, so it is sent to a vertical centrifuge, also called a separator or a finisher, for one final spin at twice the velocity of the horizontal centrifuge.

The new olive oil, still turbid, needs to settle for a few months before being bottled. (The exception is *olio nuovo*, which is bottled soon after processing, but because particulate matter is still present, it should be consumed quickly.) Olive oil is stored in stainless-steel tanks in a cool room. Inert gas fills the head space to prevent oxidation, and any solids and water that collect in the bottom are removed so they don't ferment and contaminate the oil.

Because different varieties of olives ripen at different times, growers often mill batches of single varietals or from specific orchards separately. This lets them blend olive oils to their liking, mixing greener oil from an earlier harvest with oil that is riper and more mellow, or mixing oil with a stronger taste profile together with a more delicate one. A skillful blender, working with good lots of extra-virgin oil, can produce finished olive oils with complex character.

Some producers filter their olive oil, but most do not, thinking that polyphenols, and therefore flavor, are lost through filtering.

Bottling is the last step of the journey from olive tree to olive oil. Some bottles travel to retail stores, others are sent to customers through direct sales. All will end up in kitchens to help food taste its best.

A BRIEF HISTORY OF AMERICAN OLIVE OIL

In 1997, Ridgely Evers's DaVero extra-virgin olive oil, produced in northern California, won a blind tasting in Italy. This triumph was a result of a revival of the American olive oil industry that began in the 1980s. Instead of making bulk oils, olive oil makers shifted the focus and aimed to make high-quality olive oil that would rival the best in the world. To this end, they revived old trees planted decades before, imported new trees from Europe, and sought advice from Europeans who had been making high-quality oil much longer. The trend continues today, with more acreage planted and more extra-virgin olive oil produced each year. But it wasn't always this way. Trees brought by the missionaries were neglected, economic conditions and imports affected the domestic market, and a demand for canned olives made oil less important. Now the American olive oil industry is back on track and prospering.

Olive trees came to the New World from Seville, Spain, in the early 1500s, arriving first in Hispaniola and Cuba. Because missionary work was an important part of settling these new lands, priests were among the colonists, and they played an important role in disseminating plants. They took olive trees to Mexico City, then to Baja California, and later to Alta California, the old name for today's California.

Although settlers on the eastern seaboard also brought olive trees, mostly from Italy, only a few of the plantings were successful. Thomas Jefferson added olive trees to his extensive garden at Monticello, but they failed to thrive; the climatic conditions were wrong. Some trees, perhaps obtained from Jefferson, that Nathaniel Greene planted on Cumberland Island off the coast of Georgia, were productive from 1804 to 1886. At one point, there were six hundred of them, which may have produced as much as three thousand gallons of oil a season. Today only a few remain.

The growing conditions along the southwest coast were closer to the Mediterranean climes of the olive trees' origins. It is not clear whether the first olive trees in California were from seeds or cuttings of trees in Baja, nor is it certain exactly when they arrived. A group of Franciscan fathers led by Junípero Serra established Mission San Diego de Alcalá in 1769. Some time in the following twenty years, the padres planted olive trees; by 1803 they were pressing oil. By then there were seven missions, all cultivating olive trees. Because of where they were planted, these trees became known as Mission trees, although they are most likely a variety of Cornicabra Cornezuelo, a Spanish cultivar.

Olive production was a thriving concern until 1835, when the last of the missions passed into secular hands. With their religious caretakers gone, the orchards declined, but by 1855, ranchers started taking cuttings from the old trees to start new orchards. Ellwood Cooper and Frank Kimball—two men with no olive-growing experience but who saw a business opportunity in olive oil—planted thousands of cuttings from the Mission trees. Nurseries were established, and different olive varieties were imported, most notably Manzanillo and Sevillano trees, which would eventually outnumber the Mission trees. Along with the cultivars Ascolano and Baroni, these were important choices when the emphasis shifted from oil to canned olives.

The gold rush brought Italians to California, many from Lucca, noted for its olive oil. When the miners failed to make their fortunes, they took up other pursuits. Perhaps because they missed the olives and the oil of their homeland, many planted olive trees, sharing the olives and oil with their fellow immigrants.

When people started planting vineyards, they often grew olive trees as well, a practice that was repeated in the 1980s when the latest revival of California olive oil began.

The post-gold-rush olive oil renewal suffered setbacks in the late 1890s. Olive oil from Italy, Spain, and France had always been imported into the country. In response to the burgeoning population of California, the Europeans stepped up their exports. Their prices were lower, often due to the substitution of cheaper oils for a portion of the real thing, a practice that continues among unscrupulous processors even today. The local enterprises couldn't compete.

Another factor was the emergence, in 1900, of a new cooking oil with a low price. David Wesson figured out how to deodorize cottonseed oil, making the otherwise unpalatable oil tasteless, a trait many Americans came to prefer. In 1911, Mazola, a refined oil made from corn, appeared. It too was bland, with a lower price tag than olive oil. Refined seed oils, subjected to high temperatures and harsh chemicals that strip them of many nutrients, remain popular. Even some expeller-pressed oils—in theory a healthier way to obtain oil—are taken a step further and refined. Bad olive oil, with high acidity levels or taste defects, must undergo the same treatment.

As the demand for domestic olive oil dropped, the interest in cured olives grew. Various processes can tame the extraordinary bitterness and astringency of fresh olives and make them palatable, but at the same time they were unreliable on a large scale. In 1899, George Colby and Frederic Bioletti, scientists at Berkeley's College of Agriculture, perfected a method of preserving olives in metal cans. This was the birth of the canned California black olive, a curiosity because the olives weren't naturally black. They were picked green, then chemically treated. These tasteless black ovals are still a staple of the food industry, appearing on salad bars and take-out pizzas.

Charles Gifford, working in San Diego, was the first Californian to can olives commercially. Another important player in this new industry was Freda Ehmann. A widow who lost all her financial resources when her olive orchard near Oroville flooded and the olive industry became depressed, she was determined to pay the debts she and her son had incurred to buy the orchard. The olive trees recovered, and within three years they had a crop. But she had no idea how to cure olives. She asked Eugene Hilgard, the dean of the College of Agriculture at the University of California, for advice. He supplied a formula and she went to work. Her business grew, and by 1900 she had a large processing plant in Oroville. Benefiting from the work of Colby and Bioletti, she switched to metal cans in 1905, selling olives across the country. Her business suffered a near-fatal setback in 1919 when an outbreak of botulism at a banquet in Ohio was traced to some of her olives. Although the olive canning industry improved its processing methods, it took years to regain the trust of consumers. People were wary of olive oil as well, even though it didn't carry the same risk of botulism. Then the Great Depression hit, and olives became a luxury food.

Political turmoil in Italy and Spain in the late 1930s prevented importation of olives and olive oil, so the California producers began to recover. The end of the war reopened the import trade, again making it difficult for them. Canned olives dominated the crop.

Despite the economic conditions, however, one determined family, led by Nicola Sciabica, started producing olive oil in

Modesto in 1936, spurred on by olive oil production methods learned in their native Sicily. Initially, they took the olives elsewhere to be pressed, but by 1941 they had their own equipment. They managed to stay in business through tough times, augmenting their income by maintaining vineyards and selling grapes, and are still a going concern today. During the most recent surge of olive oil production, the Sciabicas have offered advice to newcomers, and they pressed many of these new producers' oils before more mills were built.

A new interest in olive oil production began percolating in the late 1980s. The health benefits of olive oil were in the news; its monounsaturated fat made it a preferred choice over butter. Many of these pioneers were vineyard and winery owners who looked at old olive trees on their properties in a new light. Lila Jaeger, who owned the Rutherford Hill Winery in the Napa Valley, discovered very old olive trees at the back of her property. Not knowing how to revive them, she sought advice from Darrell Corti of Corti Brothers in Sacramento and George Martin at the University of California at Davis. George's expertise was table olives, so he sent her to Paul Vossen, the farm advisor for Sonoma County, who had never worked with olives but quickly started to learn about them. Others interested in getting into olive oil also started to contact Paul. Lila suggested they band together to exchange information.

The first informal meeting of what was to become the Northern California Olive Oil Council met at Rutherford Hill in July 1991. In addition to Lila and Paul, other olive oil producers—Ridgely Evers, Ed Stolman, Ken Stutz, Neil Blomquist, Greg Reisinger, and Nick Sciabica—were involved. People in other parts of the state were interested in knowledge of olive oil production too, so by 1992 the group had dropped "Northern" from its name and become the California Olive Oil Council.

Some of the producers had vineyards; others focused only on olives, bringing in trees from Europe and planting orchards. Their aim was to produce high-quality olive oil. In some ways there are parallels with the California wine industry. Rustic wines became more sophisticated; small wineries concentrating on quality instead of quantity expanded; eventually, California wine won the famous tasting in Paris in 1976, trumping French wine.

Paul Vossen helped the California Olive Oil Council establish a taste panel in 1997, adhering to the guidelines set forth by the International Olive Oil Council. (The name has since been changed to the International Olive Council to reflect its inclusion of table olives.) The panel members were trained to perceive defects as well as positive attributes in olive oil. Producers could submit their oils for organoleptic evaluation in blind tasting sessions to evaluate the flavors, tastes, and aromas of the oil. If an oil met the California Olive Oil Council standards, the producer could display a seal on the bottle stating that it qualified for extra-virgin status. In 2008, 172 earned the seal—a considerable increase from the twenty-nine oils certified in 1998.

The California Olive Oil Council Seal Certification program for California extra-virgin olive oil has two components. Olive oils are submitted for laboratory analysis and must have an acidity level of less than 0.5 percent (lower than the International Olive Council standard of 0.8) and demonstrate a low level of primary oxidation.

The olive oil must also be tasted by at least eight members of a trained panel. If a majority of the tasters find the oil defect-free and possessing some fruity characteristics, it can be called extra-virgin. These are blind tastings. Because color is not a good indicator of an olive oil's quality, the samples are presented in cobalt-blue glasses that obscure their hue. The glasses are heated to about 82 degrees Fahrenheit, a temperature that maximizes the flavor components' volatilization so they can be better perceived. Each is evaluated in silence before moving on to the next. Not until each taster completes a score sheet and the sheets are collected is an olive oil discussed. The only information given about the oil is the varietal mix of olives, the harvest date, and the general growing area—the tasters never learn the producer's name.

As more acreage was planted with olive trees, the need for olive mills increased. New ones were built; the distance from orchard to mill shrank, allowing speedier processing. By 2008, thirty-six mills were operating in California.

The boutique olive oil operations continue to grow. As well as orchards with widely spaced trees that will grow tall, new orchards are being planted with semidwarf trees spaced very close together for mechanical harvesting—a technique developed by the Spanish in 1999. These super-high-density orchards are springing up in the Central Valley. The harvesting method decreases the cost, so these olive oils, which meet the California Council Olive Oil Council's extra-virgin standards, can compete with the imports at the lower end of the price range. Generally they are made in a delicate style, easing the transition to extra-virgin olive oil for people who are accustomed to bland, refined seed oils.

In each Mediterranean country where olives have been grown for centuries, certain varieties dominate. Not so here—the adventurous Americans are breaking the rules, planting cultivars from every corner of the olive-growing world. So in addition to trees typically grown in Tuscany—Frantoio, Leccino, Pendolino, and Maurino—there are plantings of Greek Koroneiki, Spanish Arbequina, and French Lucques. California producers often blend varieties together and occasionally add Mission olives to the mix.

Virtually all US olive cultivation is in California. Some trees grow in Arizona, and vintners in Oregon are experimenting with olive trees. In south Texas, commercial production began with the harvesting of the first super-high-density olive orchards in 2007.

The University of California at Davis took a significant step in supporting the olive industry when, in January 2008, it opened the Olive Center as part of the Robert Mondavi Institute for Wine and Food Science. The center brings together a wide range of disciplines to conduct academic research, provide technical support on state legislation, establish a research taste panel, plant experimental orchards, and teach courses on olive oil production and sensory evaluation.

Adulterated olive oil is still a problem, just as it was in the late 1890s. In August 2007, Tom Mueller wrote "Slippery Business" in the *New Yorker*, detailing some of the fraud that goes on. For example, hazelnut oil from one Mediterranean country might be shipped to another country, relabeled as extra-virgin olive oil, then exported. In 1998, the New York law firm Rabin and Peckel filed a class-action suit against Unilever, the manufacturer of Bertolli olive oil, alleging that their oil was labeled "imported from Italy" when it had merely passed through Italian ports after having been manufactured in Tunisia, Turkey, Spain, or Greece. The case was settled out of court in 2001. California law strives to prevent such unscrupulous practices. Any oil labeled "California Olive Oil" must be made from olives grown in the state. An oil with a California Olive Oil Council extra-virgin seal meets even more stringent requirements.

Although more olive oil is produced in California each year, the United States still imports more than 99 percent of the olive oil consumed. This imported oil ranges from exceptional extra-virgin olive oil carefully made by reputable producers to bulk oil that is at best mediocre and at worst defective. This opens opportunities for the domestic industry to educate consumers about extra-virgin olive oil as well as capture a stronger share of the market.

Labels on imported oils are a problem. The International Olive Council has strict labeling standards, but these apply only in countries that are part of the organization. The United States is not a member of the IOC, so its regulations don't apply here, tempting producers with inferior oil to label it as they wish and ship it to us.

The United States Department of Agriculture is working toward adopting the same standards as the International Olive Council, which might happen by 2009. This will make the status of imported oils more clear. Until then, the price can give a clue. Paul Vossen says that a 500-milliliter bottle of truly extra-virgin olive oil must cost at least ten dollars. The real thing is expensive to make.

Meanwhile, the California Olive Oil Council's seal on a bottle of California olive oil is the only solid assurance a consumer has that the oil is what the label says it is.

The 2007 Los Angeles International Extra-Virgin Olive Oil Competition, one of the most prestigious in the world, received 396 oils for judging from 274 producers. Sixteen countries—Argentina, Australia, Chile, France, Greece, Israel, Italy, Japan, New Zealand, Peru, Portugal, South Africa, Spain, Tunisia, Turkey, and the United States—submitted oils. California olive oils garnered 101 medals, thirty-four of them gold. In the domestic category, the best-of-show olive oils for delicate, medium, and robust styles all came from the central coast of California. In comparison, the 2008 competition received 510 oils from 334 producers. California oils received 169 medals, fifty-three of them gold.

The early missionaries started an important industry when they brought olive trees to California and pressed the fruit for oil. During the ensuing decades, table olives dominated the industry and imports provided tough competition, but now the emphasis has shifted, and American olive oil is important again. Producers range from small family concerns selling their wares at farmers' markets and boutique businesses where many owners hold other jobs or made their fortunes in other fields, to large growers and millers who see the business thriving and prospering. In 2008, California will produce about half a million gallons of olive oil, close to the entire production of France.

CLASSIFICATION AND LABELING OF OLIVE OIL
International Standards for Olive Oil

The International Olive Council revised its standards in 2007. Although the distinction between the categories may seem fuzzy, they are more useful than the US grades, which are outdated.

The International Council delineates two categories, Olive Oil and Olive Pomace Oil, with a total of nine grades in all. The oils are classified by how they were produced, by their chemistry, and by their flavor.

Olive Oil Category: This is oil solely from the fruit of the olive tree, not mixed with other kinds of oils, such as seed or nut, and not subjected to solvents or refining.

Virgin Olive Oil is obtained solely from olives by mechanical means without chemicals or excessive heat. This class is broken down into three grades that are fit for human consumption.

(1) Extra-Virgin Olive Oil is the highest grade. The oil has a laboratory-confirmed acidity level of less than 0.8 percent and has been deemed by a certified taste panel to be free of defects and to possess positive olive oil characteristics.

(2) Virgin Olive Oil is allowed an acidity level up to 2 percent and may have a defect of up to 3.5 (on a scale of 1 to 10). This level of defect is generally lower than the general population's taste threshold, but can be detected by a certified taste panel. The chemistry and flavor components distinguish this category from the general Virgin Olive Oil category, which specifies how the oil must be made.

(3) Ordinary Olive Oil, with permissible acidity of up to 3.3 percent and a defect score of up to 6, must be refined before it is fit for human consumption.

Olive Oil is a blend of refined and unrefined olive oil, with varying amounts of extra-virgin or virgin oil in the mix. It represents the bulk of the oil in the world market.

Lampante oil, with a defect greater than 6 or an acidity level more than 3.3 percent, and **Olive Oil, Not Fit For Human Consumption** are not edible oils. These oils are refined, so most or all of the defective flavors are removed, then mixed with some extra-virgin or virgin olive oil and sold as olive oil.

Olive Pomace Oil Category: This oil is obtained by treating the dregs of the olives, called the pomace, after the good oil has been extracted. There are three grades, and only one, **Olive**

Pomace Oil, is edible. It is refined pomace oil with an acidity of not more than 1 percent that has virgin oil added to provide a semblance of olive oil taste.

Inferior oil such as lampante and olive pomace oil must be refined to be fit for human consumption. But the refining process is a salvage operation; it cannot turn a poor oil into an extra-virgin olive oil.

There are several treatments that the oil undergoes in the refining process. Suspended particles are removed by settling and degumming (treating the oil with water and phosphoric acid). Next, the free fatty acids are neutralized by treating the oil with sodium hydroxide, which bonds with the fatty acids to form soap, which is then removed. Decolorization is next, accomplished by subjecting the oil to activated carbon and absorbent clays. Deodorization, accomplished by running the oil over steam in a vacuum tower at temperatures as high as 445 degrees Fahrenheit, removes volatiles, sterols, pigments, and tocopherols. (The International Olive Council allows the addition of alpha-tocopherol to refined oil because the treatment strips the oil of this valuable component.) Winterization removes high-melting-point glycerides that may cause clouding by chilling the oil to just above freezing, then filtering it. The refining process renders the oil completely flavorless. It becomes a manufactured product, bearing no resemblance to the fruit that produced it.

All seed oils, with the exception of those that are only expeller pressed, must be extracted by a refining process like the one described above. Sometimes even harsher chemicals, such as the petroleum-based hexane solvent, are also employed. These oils, just like their refined olive oil cousins, are also manufactured, not natural, products.

The International Olive Council also lists certain positive attributes that are present in extra-virgin olive oil:

Fruity: The olfactory sensations of olive oil, perceived either nasally or retronasally (that is, after the oil is swallowed), are the result of pressing sound, fresh olives and depend to some extent on the cultivar. The aroma can have many nuances. Tasters often use descriptors such as wood/hay/straw, artichoke, green tea, grass, green apple, herbaceous, tomato leaf, cinnamon, mint, nutty, tropical, floral, buttery, and apricot.

Bitter: A characteristic of olive oil perceived on the sides of the tongue in the back of the mouth. Most good olive oils have some bitterness, although it can be excessive.

Pungent: A characteristic of olive oil perceived as a peppery sensation in the throat. As with bitterness, most good olive oils will have a pungent component.

The International Olive Council also lists negative attributes that can occur in olive oil, defects that disqualify the oil as extra-virgin and that certified tasters are trained to detect. They are:

Fusty/Muddy Sediment: An aroma of anaerobic fermentation, often a problem when olives are left in piles, held too long after being picked before pressing, or left in contact with the sediment in tanks. The aroma is particularly foul, especially in advanced stages, when it is described as vomit or manure. This defect and rancidity are the most common afflictions of inexpensive oils on supermarket shelves.

Rancid: The aroma and taste of oil that has oxidized, often described as stale nuts, cardboard, or putty.

Musty/Humid: A moldy aroma and taste sometimes described as damp basement or wet cement resulting from olives that have been attacked by fungi while being stored in humid conditions. It is often more pronounced retronasally.

Winey-Vinegary/Acid/Sour: An aroma of aerobic fermentation leading to the formation of acetic acid, ethyl acetate, and ethanol, first detected as a yeasty smell then progressing to a strong acetone aroma.

Metallic: A flavor resulting from prolonged contact with reactive metals during processing. The use of stainless-steel equipment has decreased the incidence of this defect.

Other defects include:

Heated or Burnt: An off flavor caused by excessive heating during processing.

Hay-Wood: A flavor produced from dried olives.

Rough: Oil with a thick mouthfeel.

Greasy: Oil reminiscent of grease or mineral oil.

Vegetable Water: A flavor caused by prolonged contact with the water in the olives that is released during milling.

Brine: A flavor of olives preserved in brine before processing.

Esparto: A hemp-like flavor that occurs when olives were pressed on new mats.

Earthy: A flavor resulting from olives that were dirty or muddy.

Grubby: A flavor resulting from an olive fly infestation. Depending on the severity of the infestation, the taste can be fusty and/or rancid.

Cucumber: A flavor resulting from prolonged storage in tin containers.

Wet Wood: A flavor of oil made from olives injured by frost while on the tree.

United States Standards for Olive Oil

The United States Department of Agriculture standards for olive oil date from 1948. The basic premise is that it must be the edible oil from the fruit of the olive tree. It is rated on a scale of 100 with this breakdown: free fatty acid content—30 points; absence of defects—30 points; odor—20 points; and flavor—20 points. There are four categories—US Grade A, also called US Fancy; US Grade B, or US Choice; US Grade C, or US Standard; and US Grade D, or Substandard.

There is a great flaw in this system. Solid criteria for determining absence of defects, odor, and flavor, which account for 70 of the 100 possible points, are missing. In other words, a sensory evaluation component—including who will evaluate it and how—is not part of this grading system. And since American olive oil producers don't use these terms on their labels, they are effectively irrelevant.

The California Olive Oil Council has proposed that the USDA adopt the International Olive Council standards. This idea is slowly working its way through the government mechanism. Laboratory analysis is not a problem, but a method to meet the requirements of sensory analysis remains to be developed.

Another important necessity, according to Paul Vossen, the farm advisor in Sonoma and Marin counties, is the establishment of a "marketing order." These orders are governed by the Marketing Order Administrative Board. The board supports a set of laws defined by an industry that would enforce standards and aid research and promotion. Such an order requires the approval of two thirds of the domestic growers representing two thirds of the sales volume. A movement to include imported oils in the standard requires a vote of Congress.

California Standards for Olive Oil

A law delineating particulars for the labeling of olive oil in California was enacted in 1997. The sale of imitation olive oil—that is, any edible oil artificially altered to resemble olive oil—is not allowed, although the blending of other edible oils with olive oil is permitted, as long as it is not labeled "olive oil".

Any oil labeled "California Olive Oil" must be made from olives grown in the state. Olive oils labeled as coming from an approved viticultural area (for example, "Napa Valley Olive Oil") must contain at least 75 percent oil made from olives grown in the designated area.

In 2007, a bill was put before the California legislature that upgrades the description of olive oil and extra-virgin olive oil and will replicate the International Olive Council and California Olive Oil Council proposed USDA standards. Governor Schwarzenegger signed this bill in 2008 and it went into effect in January of 2009.

CHOOSING AND STORING EXTRA-VIRGIN OLIVE OIL

A friend recently asked me to accompany her to an independent high-end grocery store where she often shops to choose a bottle of olive oil. There was a large selection, both of imported oils and those made in California. Without any knowledge of what was in the bottle, it was difficult for her to make a decision. I suggested she narrow her search by following a few guidelines, which can apply for both imported and domestic olive oils.

Limit the choice to oils labeled extra-virgin. Olive oil labeled pure or light is refined oil, which is tasteless on its own, so producers add a little bit of extra-virgin olive oil for flavor. ("Light" means lightly flavored, not low-calorie—the oil has the same number of calories as extra-virgin olive oil.) Unfortunately, imported oil labeled extra-virgin is not a reliable indication of an oil's quality because of lax labeling laws.

The phrase "first cold press" is a throwback to the days when olives were pressed between mats, often more than once. For subsequent pressings, the paste was heated in order to extract more oil. With the sophisticated machinery used today to make extra-virgin olive oil, the olive paste or the oil itself is never heated above 86 degrees Fahrenheit, so the term is meaningless unless the oil was actually produced in a press.

Choose oils packed in dark glass or in a box and stored in a cool place. Heat, light, and oxygen are enemies of olive oil, promoting oxidation and rancidity. Even superior oil will eventually go rancid due to slow oxidation. Retail shelves are often lit by stark lights that produce heat or may even be exposed to sunlight. Dark bottles or some outside covering like a box help protect the oil. But many curious consumers want to see the color of the oil (even though color is not an accurate indicator of quality or taste), so producers often use clear glass.

Examine the bottle for either a harvest date or a use-by date, which is usually eighteen to twenty-four months after the harvest. This may be in small lettering anywhere on the bottle, sometimes on the bottom. The more recent the harvest, the better. Good extra-virgin olive oil stored properly will keep for at least a year, although it may lose some fruitiness. (Harvest or use-by dates are not popular with retailers because knowledgeable customers might decide against buying an olive oil that is a year old.) Olives are harvested in the fall and winter and are generally allowed to settle before bottling. (The exception is *olio nuovo*, which is sold shortly after it is milled.) This means that an olive oil sold in the late fall and early winter is one year old. The way the olive oil was stored makes a difference in its soundness. Some producers are forgoing distributors and retail markets, instead selling their olive oil bottled to order exclusively to restaurants or on the Internet because they have more control over quality.

Price does matter. Extra-virgin olive oil, especially if it is hand-harvested, is expensive to produce. Be wary of extra-virgin olive oils selling for less than twenty dollars a liter, and ask questions if an oil's price is drastically reduced. Some people raise their eyebrows at the price of a good extra-virgin olive oil, but those same people might pay even more for a fine bottle of wine that is consumed in an evening.

If the label on a bottle of olive oil sports a medal from a fair or competition, it means that a trained panel tasted it and found it distinctive. The medal should include the year that it was awarded and correspond with the harvest or use-by date on the bottle.

In the best of worlds, you can taste an olive oil before buying. Some producers have installed olive oil bars in retail stores, and some specialty shops have olive oils for tasting.

Once your selection is made, you must store it properly, preferably in a cool, dark place. Refrigeration can be harmful— each time the bottle is removed from the cold, condensation can form on the inside of the lid and drop into the oil, introducing oxygen. It is tempting to keep oil next to the stove (I recently saw a photograph from a national food magazine that showed oils stored on a shelf suspended from the ceiling directly over the stove burners), but prolonged exposure to high temperatures will foster rancidity. Match the size of the bottle to your needs. How much will you consume in two months? Olive oil in large bottles should be transferred to smaller containers when it is half gone to decrease oxygen exposure. And finally, do not save an olive oil for special occasions. It will not improve with age.

After careful consideration, my friend chose McEvoy in a light-protected bottle with a recent harvest date that had a current certification seal from the California Olive Oil Council—a good choice.

EXTRA-VIRGIN OLIVE OIL IN THE KITCHEN

Use only extra-virgin olive oil in your kitchen. There are three styles of extra-virgin olive oil—delicate, medium, and robust— that you will want to have available all the time. All olive oils should be fruity. Their bitterness and pungency will vary, determining the styles into which they fall. Each recipe in this book suggests a suitable style of extra-virgin olive oil or a flavored olive oil for the desired result.

Sometimes the varieties of olives are mentioned on the label, and this can help you choose a style. Although styles are influenced by growing, harvest, and processing methods, in general, oils made from Arbequina, Ascolano, Leccino, Pendolino, Maurino, and Sevillano olives are more delicate. (Leccino, Pendolino, and Maurino are Tuscan olive varietals that are often blended with more assertive Tuscan-style olives.) Delicate oils have some bitterness and pungency but are mild, either because of the olive variety or the age of the olives when picked. If they are from more mature olives, they may have buttery, nutty, or sweet tones. Oils from Ascolano and Sevillano olives tend to be delicate but very fruity with tropical and floral aromas.

Medium-style olive oils have a pleasant bitterness and pungency and tend to be very versatile. The best of these olive oils have characteristics of both delicate and robust oils. Oils made with French olive varietals, such as Aglandau and Bouteillon, or from the Spanish Hojiblanca, tend to be in the medium style.

Many medium olive oils are blends of delicate and robust oils.

Robust olive oils are cough-producing. Many people laud this characteristic, considering it a sign of superior oil; others find it too aggressive. Flavor this assertive goes very well with some things and can overwhelm others. These olive oils have the highest levels of polyphenols (chemical antioxidant compounds), which are responsible for their robustness, and they will last longer than either a delicate or a medium oil. The bitterness and pungency will fade with time. The Tuscan olive varietals Frantoio and Moraiolo, as well as the Spanish Arbosana and the Greek Koroneiki typically produce robust oils.

In California many oils are made from Mission or Manzanillo olives, once grown for canning. Oils made from Mission olives can vary considerably, depending on the harvest date. When picked green, Mission olive oil is very bitter (robust); if harvested at midseason, it is fruity with some bitterness and pungency (medium); a late-harvest Mission olive makes a buttery and rather mild oil (delicate).

Manzanillo olive oil can be fruity and peppery with woody overtones and usually falls into either the medium or robust category.

Oils made from Ascolano or Sevillano olives have distinct flavor profiles. They have intense aromas—tropical, apricot, pineapple—and very little bitterness and pungency.

Flavored olive oils, which by definition cannot be called extra-virgin because they contain other things beside olives, also have a place in the kitchen. For a long time, they were considered outcasts by serious olive oil producers, but now they are viewed more favorably. (Nine flavored olive oils were awarded medals at the 2002 Los Angeles Competition; in 2007, twenty-eight flavored oils achieved medal status.) The best are made following the same guidelines used to make extra-virgin olive oil, because the flavoring will not mask a defective oil.

The combination that I think works best is the citrus oils. Either the whole fruit or just the peel is crushed right along with the olives, or an essential citrus oil is added to the malaxation tank. Flavorings added after the oil is made (these are called infused oils) are often harsh with a chemical taste. A taster once described a lemon-infused oil as tasting like Lemon Pledge.

Some herb oils are also useful, particularly if the plant is crushed with the olives, although some can be overpowering. Avoid oils with steeped raw garlic or other fresh herbs or vegetables because they are susceptible to botulism.

The flavor of extra-virgin olive oil is best when it is heated gently or not at all, so I have offered recipes in this book that allow the taste of the olive oil to shine. Heating extra-virgin olive oil will reduce some of the fruitiness, but it still retains its characteristics, so I have specified styles of oils in the cooked recipes. If you have an extra-virgin olive oil that is too bitter or pungent for your taste, use it to sauté.

Extra-virgin olive oil (not your most expensive bottle) can be used for deep-frying in a home kitchen, where the frying temperature does not exceed 375 degrees Fahrenheit and the oil doesn't smoke. After cooling and straining, the oil can be used for deep frying once more.

I was skeptical the first time I made a pound cake with extra-virgin olive oil instead of butter and was pleasantly surprised at the results. When baking, use this general substitution rule: Use three fourths the amount of extra-virgin olive oil as butter, that is, instead of eight ounces of butter, use six ounces of oil. Many people use only delicate olive oils for baking, but I have found that citrus oils and even some robust oils serve nicely.

Many producers call their extra-virgin olive oils condiment oils—they are not for cooking but to drizzle on foods after they are cooked or on foods that aren't cooked at all. Unless people are from an ethnic background where olive oil was a staple, the notion of pouring oil on a piece of cooked fish or meat may seem strange. But the practice can enhance the flavor. Use your most complex extra-virgin olive oils as condiment oils. At a food pairing I once attended, a rather delicate extra-virgin olive oil, with ripe olive characteristics and a little pungency, brought out the sweetness of a delicious osso bucco. The same style of oil can improve a tomato that is not quite ripe.

Sometimes traditional food pairings are not the best. At that same tasting I tried a delicate, ripe extra-virgin olive oil that should theoretically have paired well with cooked beans. They tasted flat. Another olive oil with a little more piquancy brought out the flavor. Many people prefer a delicate extra-virgin olive oil for mayonnaise, while an aïoli, rich in garlic, needs an oil with some bitterness and pungency. Bitter greens should pair with a robust extra-virgin olive oil, but if both elements are assertive, the flavors may compete, not complement each other. A more delicate olive oil might be a better match. Ideally, the taste of the oil and the taste of the food add up to a sum better than the parts. Try different combinations to see what you prefer.

AN EXTRA-VIRGIN OLIVE OIL AND FOOD PAIRING TASTING

An enjoyable way to explore the nuances of matching extra-virgin olive oils with food, as well as appreciating the differences in individual preferences, is to host a blind tasting lunch. First the guests taste the olive oils alone; then they mix and match them with a plate of food, taking note of which oil they prefer with each food selection.

Because cooked foods absorb oil better when they are warm, prepare the foods for the tasting close to serving time. Serve each guest a plate with warm food—a spoonful of cooked cannellini beans, a boiled potato, a few slices of poached chicken breast, and a few slices of grilled flank steak. Also serve a mound of tender salad greens on a second plate, along with a slice of bread (not sourdough), a few slices of mozzarella cheese, two or three slices of tomato (hopefully vine-ripened), and a few slivers of Parmesan cheese. Serve water during this exercise. Provide wine and Walnut-Rosemary Biscotti (see recipe, p. 198) to reward the participants after the tasting is over.

To prepare the cooked foods:

Soak dried cannellini beans, about a tablespoon per person, overnight in cold water. The next day, drain them, add fresh water to cover by two inches, bring to a simmer, and cook over low heat until the beans are tender, about one hour. Salt the cooking liquid to taste. Leave the beans in the cooking liquid until serving time, reheating them if necessary.

Boil small waxy potatoes, one per person, in salted water until tender. Drain and keep warm.

Put chicken breasts, enough for each person to have two or three slices, skin and bone attached, into a pot and cover with cold water. Bring to a simmer and skim. Add aromatics—a carrot, half an onion, a celery stalk, a few parsley sprigs, salt, and a few whole black peppercorns—and simmer until the chicken registers 140 degrees Fahrenheit on an instant-read thermometer, fifteen to twenty minutes, depending on the size. Remove it from the pot, cut from the bone, slice, and serve.

Generously salt and pepper a flank steak (preferably grass-fed), enough for each person to have two or three slices. Prepare a hardwood charcoal fire. Grill the steak over a hot fire, turning it once. The time will depend on the thickness. An inch-thick steak will take three to four minutes per side. Check the temperature with an instant-read thermometer; it should read 120 degrees Fahrenheit for rare meat. Remove the steak from the grill, loosely cover it with foil, and let it rest for five minutes. Cut it into quarter-inch slices across the grain and serve.

Choose three of your favorite extra-virgin olive oils—a delicate, a medium, and a robust. If you have dark-colored drinking glasses, set three at each place along with a waterglass. Lacking colored glasses, use brandy snifters or wineglasses. Write numbers on the bases of the glasses with a removable marker. At each place, fill one glass with about two tablespoons of delicate extra-virgin olive oil, the second with two tablespoons of medium extra-virgin olive oil, and the third with the same amount of robust extra-virgin olive oil. Keep the order the same at each setting. Cover the glasses with coasters or pieces of paper. Fill the waterglasses and put a small bowl of apple slices beside each setting.

Pour more of each of the extra-virgin olive oils into cruets, number them to correspond to the oil in the glasses, and put them on the table, along with salt and a peppermill. Supply each place with notepaper and a pencil. Don't reveal any information about the extra-virgin olive oils until the tasting is over.

Before bringing the food to the table, have the guests taste each oil and record their impressions on paper, starting with the delicate oil. To taste, uncover and pick up the glass, cup the bowl or bottom in one hand, cover the top with the other hand and gently swirl the glass to heat the olive oil until the glass no longer feels cold. Then inhale deeply with the nose very close to the glass. Note the intensity of the aroma. Is it noticeable or faint? Does it smell green, like freshly mowed grass, straw, artichoke, mint, green banana, green tea, or tomato leaf? Or does it smell ripe—nutty, buttery, floral? Perhaps it has both green and ripe aromas. Next think of the taste. Tip about a teaspoon of olive oil into the mouth. Suck in air and swirl the olive oil around. Swallow, then breathe out through the nose. Do any of the aromas translate into the taste? Note the degree of bitterness, perceived at the back of the mouth, and pungency, felt as a peppery sensation in the throat. Is the oil cough-producing? Is it astringent, producing a drying sensation in the mouth? How long do these sensations last? What is the mouthfeel—is it thin or greasy? Take a few sips of water, a few bites of apple, and wait a minute or two before tasting the next olive oil.

After each person has some general impressions about each olive oil, serve the food.

Now the real fun begins. Ask the guests to try each of the food selections with each of the olive oils to see which match they prefer, taking notes as they taste. When all the olive oils have been paired and the food has disappeared, ask people to state their preferences. Then reveal the names and styles of the olive oils. There may be some surprises. When I have conducted this exercise at sensory evaluation courses given by the University of California Extension Service, there was rarely a match that everyone preferred. At one course, a slim majority liked the potato with a robust Tuscan blend from California; a California Arbequina oil—whose taste profile is the opposite of a Tuscan-style oil—was a close second. Some people had a hardwired preference for a particular style of olive oil and liked it with everything.

One outcome is certain. People will learn more about extra-virgin olive oil styles and which styles they prefer.

OLIVE OIL AND HEALTH

The Mediterranean diet, long considered a healthy one, has some distinct characteristics. It includes a high consumption of grains, cereals, fresh fruits, legumes, vegetables, nuts, and seeds. Dairy products, fish, and poultry are consumed in moderate amounts. What little red meat is consumed tends to be from animals that were grass-fed. Wine is drunk almost daily in moderate amounts. Olive oil is the major source of fat. Although many components of the diet are thought to be responsible for its healthy profile, olive oil is a major contributor.

Numerous scientific studies of the Mediterranean diet have been conducted over the last few decades. A recent book, *More on Mediterranean Diets*, edited by A. P. Simopoulos and F. Visioli, summarizes this research and is a rich source of up-to-date information.

Various compounds in olive oil contribute to its healthy aspects. Oleic acid, which makes up 80 percent of the fat in olive oil, is a monounsaturated fat with many cardiovascular benefits. A diet high in oleic acid (and low in saturated fat) increases the resistance of low-density lipoproteins (LDLs, the bad cholesterol) to oxidation that makes them more harmful. It also decreases the amount of LDL in the body without decreasing high-density lipoproteins (HDLs, the good cholesterol). In addition, oleic acid is beneficial in decreasing the incidence of atherosclerosis and thrombosis. Diabetics, at risk for cardiovascular disease, can benefit from olive oil's cardiovascular protective profile.

Other heart-healthy components of olive oil are the polyphenols, which act as antioxidants. Extra-virgin olive oil contains more polyphenols than other olive oils. These antioxidants circulate in the body, hooking up with free radicals, unstable compounds thought to play a role in more than sixty different health conditions including cancer and atherosclerosis, as well as aging. In addition to the polyphenols, olive oil contains tocopherols, fat-soluble vitamins that also have antioxidant properties. All these compounds also protect the oil itself from oxidation, a decomposition that leads to rancidity. Oxidized oil loses nutritional value because some of the fatty acids and fat-soluble vitamins are destroyed.

Olive oil as part of a Mediterranean diet may protect against cancers of the colon. Colon cancer mortality rates in Greece are low, even though fat intake in the form of olive oil is high. The same can be said for breast cancer —Greek women have lower rates of breast cancer than American women. Both consume about the same amount of fat with a major distinction: In Greece the fat is olive oil; in America the fat is in other forms, including saturated. Another study in Italy found an inverse association between breast cancer and consumption of seed and olive oils. The authors postulate that a two-tablespoon increase in daily olive oil consumption would confer a 10 percent decrease in risk. And as for prostate cancer, although no studies to date have looked at the relationship of olive oil consumption and this type of cancer, prostate cancer has historically been lower in countries with a high olive oil intake.

Oleocanthal, another compound present in olive oil, is in part responsible for the pungency in olive oil. It has the same properties as ibuprofen, the over-the-counter antiinflammatory drug. Perhaps a few tablespoons of olive oil (extra-virgin, of course) a day will replace the apple in keeping the doctor away.

UC DAVIS OLIVE OIL

University of California at Davis
Division of Buildings and Grounds
1 Shields Avenue
Davis, California 95616
530 752 6741
www.oliveoil.ucdavis.edu

As director of building and grounds at the University of California campus in Davis, California, Sal Genito knew the hazard well. Olive trees between a well-used bike path and Russell Boulevard, the busy street that borders one side of the campus, were once again dropping their ripe, oily fruit, staining the path and making it slick. As he saw yet another bicyclist crash to the pavement, he had a eureka moment—one akin to "if life gives you lemons, make lemonade." Rather than cleaning the path when the trees shed their fruit, why not keep ahead of the dropping olives by picking them and making oil? It would probably be more economical than the maintenance, to say nothing of the costs incurred when people were hurt.

Sal began to talk up his idea. A mutual friend led him to Dan Flynn, a political analyst working at the capital in Sacramento, who was intrigued by olives and hoped to buy property with trees one day. Sal suggested that Dan do a feasibility study. If the plan made sense, work could begin. The first batch of UC Davis olive oil was about eighty gallons. Rather than pay Dan in oil, the initial deal the two men had made, Dan suggested that Sal hire him to run the olive oil program, so Dan traded his office at the capital for space in a trailer behind the homey cottage that houses the buildings and grounds department on the campus.

The hundred and fifty trees that line Russell Boulevard are only a fraction of the olive trees on the campus. There are fifteen hundred in all, some along jogging paths, others in straight rows that probably marked boundaries before the university owned the land, and some sequestered in an experimental orchard. The most impressive stand, planted in 1861, lines a driveway that led to the estate of John Wolfskill, an early California pioneer who received a sizable land grant in 1843. These trees look almost otherworldly, with fissured trunks and tall canopies. Wolfskill's granddaughter willed 107 acres to the university, including two hundred trees, half Mission, half other varieties. In 1946, John Whisler, under the direction of professor of pomology Hudson Hartmann, grafted a hundred varieties of olives from more than twenty countries onto the old trees. These are the trees that are harvested and pressed into the Wolfskill blend. There are so few of each variety that the olives are milled together. The amount of fruit that the trees bear varies from year to year; some years there wasn't enough of a variety to include. The 2008 oil was a mix of sixty varieties; in 2006, the Wolfskill blend contained about eighty, surely the only olive oil in the world made from so many cultivars.

The 2006 harvest was sparse, only forty-five gallons. Nonetheless, it took a gold medal at the Los Angeles County Fair (since renamed the Los Angeles International Competition) that year.

The university sells two other oils. Gunrock, a more robust oil, commemorates the campus mascot, a thoroughbred horse brought to the university in 1921 to sire horses for the US Cavalry. The third, Silo, is named for a campus landmark and comprises oil from five varieties typically planted in California by the early settlers.

Since the university is new to olive oil making, it hires a special crew at harvest time. Sal did buy a used shaker to dislodge the fruit from the trees. It balked and needed coaxing to do its task the first year, but the harvest went smoother the second time around.

After harvesting, the fruit is quickly transported to Oroville, where it is milled and stored. It is bottled as demand dictates and then trucked to the campus bookstore, the only retail location where the oil is sold. (It can also be purchased on the university's web site.)

Dan Flynn has his hands full. In October 2007, he was appointed executive director of the newly formed University of California at Davis Olive Center. Meanwhile, the trees need to be pruned; many are not irrigated; there is no olive fly abatement program in place. He's been working the numbers. The university's expenditures are less than before the program started, mainly because less money is going for injury costs and cleanup. By 2009 the program may be profitable. Olive oil has become the university's lemonade.

FIGUEROA FARMS

1833 Fletcher Way
Santa Ynez, California 93460
805 686 4890
www.figueroafarms.com

Rolling hills and majestic plateaus led the way to Figueroa Mountain, the namesake of the Figueroa Farms olive ranch. Patches of grape vines were interspersed with horse pastures enclosed in wooden fences; one large equestrian establishment had its own oval track. Just as I was beginning to wonder where the olive trees were, I crested a ridge and spotted them. Their silver leaves and graceful silhouettes stood out from the deep green of the vines.

Shawn and Antoinette Addison, the owners, live in a stone house surrounded by their organic orchard and a terrace of lavender bushes. They became interested in growing olives after inheriting a ten-acre mature olive orchard and house in the south of France. Both are graduates of the Food Research Institute at Stanford University, and growing olives brought them closer to the land.

It's a short walk from the house to the mill building. Shawn, a lanky man dressed in shorts and a polo shirt, greeted me at the door and led

the way. The harvest had not yet begun, so the machinery was quiet. During harvest, it runs from four A.M. to seven P.M. most days.

Shawn was clearly proud of the equipment, a two-phase Pieralisi hammer mill, and they make the most out of that mill. In addition to their own production, they crush olives for others, even providing bottling and packaging services. This extra part of the business provides important revenues. Distribution is competitive and expensive.

The initial goal was to be a high-end supplier for Southern California, but the Addisons actually sell more oil in the northern part of the state. When Figueroa put in its mill in 2002, it was considered large. But with the growth of the industry, more mills are being built, some much bigger. Figueroa's one-ton-an-hour Pieralisi now puts the company in the boutique milling category.

The first year they had the mill, they purchased some Ascolano olives, just to learn how to use the machine; they didn't intend to sell the oil. But some people tasted it and said, "Don't throw this away." Now they make a blend of California varietals called Camino al Cielo that includes some Ascolano. It won a gold medal at the Los Angeles competition in 2004, 2005, and 2006 and a silver in 2007. They make other award-winning oils from Italian varietals.

That first milling year, they underestimated the amount of pomace—the solids left after the oil is removed—that they would produce. They had purchased containers to collect it so it could be returned to the fields, but filled them in an hour's time. Next they moved the mass into much larger containers, but the collection was still too slow. Now they collect the pomace in debris bins and sell it to a composting company.

Shawn and Antoinette travel to Provence frequently to check on the olive trees there. The week after my visit they were off to see how the fruit was ripening. There the harvest and milling are very much old-world—Shawn is still trying to convince the French workers that picking up olives from the ground is not the way to harvest.

As I was leaving I asked him how he uses their oil in cooking. "We use it anytime fat is needed. Well, maybe except for breakfast toast."

APPETIZERS AND SMALL PLATES

Small dishes are so popular today that you can't have too many in your cooking repertoire. The recipes that follow are very versatile; they can be served as snacks, with aperitifs, as first courses, or even as light lunches.

Bruschette

Bruschette require high-quality, preferably artisanal bread made with a natural starter and not too aggressively sour. Half-inch slices of bread, either grilled over charcoal or toasted, take on different personalities depending on the type of olive oil and the toppings used. Here are just a few of the many possibilities. I'm always amazed that something so simple can taste so good.

Fleur de sel, salt that is hand-raked from the top of shallow beds of seawater, has been harvested off the French coasts of Charente and Southern Brittany for centuries. When less expensive commercial salt became available after World War II, the popularity of fleur de sel declined. Nowadays its intense, mineral-rich taste is once again appreciated, and it is readily available, often in supermarkets. It adds a burst of flavor to these bruschette.

I suggest two slices of bread per serving for the simplest bruschette and only one for those that have toppings.

CATALAN TOMATO BREAD

4 SERVINGS

¼ cup (2 ounces) delicate extra-virgin olive oil

8 slices grilled or toasted bread

2 vine-ripened juicy red tomatoes

fleur de sel and freshly ground black pepper

These are served in almost every tapas bar in Barcelona. Traditionally, both sides of the bread are rubbed with olive oil and tomatoes, but I find that the oil and tomato juice soaks through, so treating one side is adequate. Make these only when tomatoes are at their best.

1. Brush the olive oil onto the bread with a pastry brush. Cut the tomatoes in half crosswise. Rub the cut side of a tomato onto each bread slice until the bread is red and moist. Sprinkle with fleur de sel and a few grindings of pepper, and serve immediately.

GARLIC BRUSCHETTA

4 SERVINGS

8 slices grilled or toasted bread

2 large garlic cloves, peeled and cut into halves

1/4 cup (2 ounces) robust extra-virgin olive oil

fleur de sel and freshly ground black pepper

Here's a chance to use a very robust extra-virgin olive oil, such as an *olio nuovo*. This oil, sold shortly after it is milled, announces a new olive oil season. It is fresh, typically bitter and robust, and cloudy because the fine particles that escaped the centrifuge remain suspended. This gives the oil a unique character but shortens its shelf life because the particles can degrade and deteriorate the oil. *Olio nuovo* typically doesn't show up in stores; buy it directly from the producers. Store it in a cool, dark place and use it within a few months.

1. Vigorously rub one side of each slice of bread with garlic. Generously brush each piece with olive oil. Sprinkle with fleur de sel and a few grindings of pepper, and serve immediately.

MUSTARD GREENS BRUSCHETTA

4 SERVINGS

4 slices grilled or toasted bread

1/4 cup (2 ounces) robust extra-virgin olive oil, divided

2 garlic cloves, peeled and sliced

6 ounces young red mustard greens, stacked, rolled, and cut into julienne

fine sea salt

fleur de sel and freshly ground black pepper

I prefer the mustard greens that have some red coloring. If you have garden space, these are very easy to grow, letting you pick the leaves while they are young and tender. If the leaves are older and have noticeable ribs, remove them.

1. Generously brush the bread with half the olive oil.

2. Heat the remaining oil in a medium skillet over high heat until it trembles, becomes aromatic, and easily coats the bottom of the pan. Add the garlic and greens. Sprinkle with fine sea salt. Lower the heat to medium and cover the skillet. Cook, stirring occasionally, until the greens are wilted, about 4 minutes. Taste the greens. If they are too crunchy, add a little water and continue cooking until they are done to your liking.

3. Top the bread with the greens, sprinkle with fleur de sel and a few grindings of pepper, and serve immediately.

CARAMELIZED ONION AND BALSAMIC VINEGAR BRUSCHETTA

4 SERVINGS

6 tablespoons extra-virgin olive oil, divided

2 large onions (about 2 pounds), peeled, halved, and thinly sliced

fine sea salt

balsamic vinegar to taste

4 slices grilled or toasted bread

fleur de sel and freshly ground black pepper

Because these caramelized onions are so deeply flavored, any style of extra-virgin olive oil is suitable for this recipe. Be patient while cooking the onions. Long, slow cooking renders them sweet with a lasting flavor. You can prepare them ahead, if you wish.

And do use your best balsamic vinegar. The intensity of balsamic vinegar varies; add it drop by drop until it imparts a complexity to the onions, but not enough so they taste of vinegar.

1. Heat 4 tablespoons of the oil in a large skillet over high heat until it trembles, becomes aromatic, and easily coats the bottom of the pan. Add the onions and turn the heat to very low. Sprinkle with salt. Cook the onions uncovered, stirring occasionally, until they are the color of a polished mahogany table, about 1 hour. They will shrink dramatically.

2. Transfer the onions to a bowl and let them cool. Add balsamic vinegar drop by drop until the flavor of the onions is complex but not vinegary. Sprinkle with fleur de sel if needed.

3. Brush the bread with the remaining 2 tablespoons oil.

4. Put a generous pile of onions on each slice of bread. Add a few grindings of pepper, and serve immediately.

TWO CHÈVRES WITH EXTRA-VIRGIN OLIVE OIL AND TOPPINGS

THE SERVING SIZE VARIES WITH THE NUMBER OF GUESTS

fresh, soft goat cheese, 1½ ounces per person

aged, more pungent goat cheese, such as a crottin, 1½ ounces per person

bread and crackers

about 4 ounces of delicate extra-virgin olive oil

about 4 ounces of robust extra-virgin olive oil

about 2 tablespoons toasted sesame seeds

about 2 tablespoons dried chili pepper flakes

about 2 tablespoons interesting freshly ground pepper, such as red Pondicherry or cubeb, if you have any

This is more of a suggestion than a recipe (if you have favorite cheeses, use them, look for rustic bread or crackers, and change the spices if you wish).

1. Put the cheeses on a board. Arrange the bread and crackers in a basket. Pour the oil in cruets and bring them to the table along with the spices in small dishes.

2. Each person can help themselves to the cheeses and breads, drizzle them with the olive oils, and add condiments as they wish. Or they can spread the cheese on bread and crackers and top with oil.

GUACAMOLE WITH PERSIAN LIME OLIVE OIL

1½ CUPS

2 ripe avocados

¼ teaspoon fine sea salt

freshly ground black pepper

⅛ teaspoon ground cayenne pepper

2 tablespoons finely chopped onion

3 tablespoons finely chopped fresh cilantro

1½ tablespoons (¾ ounce) Persian lime olive oil

2 tablespoons (1 ounce) fresh lime juice

Persian limes, also called Tahitian limes, are larger than Key limes. They are virtually seedless, juicy, and vibrantly flavored. Many people love Persian lime olive oil but are unsure how to pair it with food. It is a natural match with avocado and is the secret ingredient in this recipe, adding smoothness as well as flavor. (Persian lime olive oil also goes well on a beet salad.)

1. Peel the avocados and discard the pits. Put them in a medium bowl and sprinkle them with salt, a few grindings of black pepper, and cayenne pepper. Work them with a potato masher until they are smooth but still contain a few lumps. Add the onion, cilantro, olive oil, and lime juice and mix using a stirring motion with the potato masher.

2. If you will not be serving the guacamole immediately, put it in bowl, cover with plastic wrap directly in contact with the guacamole, and refrigerate. It is best served the day it is made.

3. Bring the guacamole to room temperature before serving.

PAN BAGNAT

4 SANDWICHES

4 round rolls, or a baguette cut into 6-inch pieces, or 6-inch squares of scallion and rosemary focaccia (see recipe, p. 166)

6 tablespoons (3 ounces) medium or robust extra-virgin olive oil

3 ounces tuna, either canned or poached in extra-virgin olive oil (see recipe, p. 115)

8 anchovy filets, either packed in olive oil or *crudo* packed in salt (see recipe, p. 123), rinsed and patted dry

1 small onion, peeled and thinly sliced

2 red bell peppers, charred, with skin, ribs, and seeds removed, or 4 roasted piquillo peppers from a jar

1/2 cup (2 ounces by weight) pitted Niçoise-style olives, rinsed and patted dry

In *The Food of France*, Waverley Root describes these sandwiches as Nice's picnic food, preferably eaten on the Mediterranean beach as a snack between dips in the sea. After the last crumb is consumed, the water can wash the oil off hands and any dribbles from the chin. If you're not on the Riviera, a picnic table and plenty of napkins will suffice.

The English translation of *pan bagnat* is "bathed bread," and the liquid used is olive oil. Typically the sandwiches contain Niçoise staples such as tomatoes, peppers, olives, sliced onions, hard-boiled eggs, radishes, anchovies, even artichoke hearts. This recipe is one rendition; you can devise your own fillings. Make them at least three hours before eating them so the oil can penetrate and flavor the bread and filling.

1. Cut the bread in half lengthwise. If you're using rolls or baguette, pull out some of the inside crumb to make more room for the filling. This isn't necessary if you're using focaccia.

2. Brush or drizzle the olive oil evenly on all 8 pieces of bread.

3. Layer the ingredients on the bottom halves and cover with the tops.

4. Tightly wrap the sandwiches in plastic wrap for at least 3 hours at a cool room temperature before serving. You can make them a day ahead and store them in the refrigerator overnight. Let them come to room temperature before serving.

PECORINO PUCKS

24 PUCKS

1 cup (5 ounces by weight) unbleached all-purpose flour

2 ounces *Pecorino pepato*, grated (about ½ cup)

½ teaspoon fine sea salt

6 tablespoons (3 ounces) extra-virgin olive oil

1 tablespoon (½ ounce) cold water

Eat these little morsels as a snack or serve them with aperitifs. The composition of the fat in olive oil contributes a crunch that isn't possible with butter's saturated fat. A *Pecorino pepato*—Pecorino with peppercorns—adds a little spice. Choose one from Italy or buy the version from Bellwether Farms, a California artisanal cheese maker.

Use any style of olive oil to make this recipe, provided that it is extra-virgin.

Because the moisture of the cheese can vary, the dough may need a little more water. If it is impossible to roll into a log, return it to the processor and, with the machine running, add one or two teaspoons of additional water.

1. Put the flour, cheese, and salt in the bowl of a food processor fitted with the metal blade.

2. With the machine running, slowly pour the oil through the feed tube, then add the water. The mixture should start to resemble dough but it will not completely adhere.

3. Turn the dough out onto a lightly floured work surface. Knead a few times until the dough is smooth. Roll it into a log about 1½ inches in diameter and 10 inches long.

4. Wrap the log in plastic wrap and refrigerate for 4 hours or up to 2 days.

5. Preheat the oven to 375°F. Put a piece of parchment paper on a baking pan.

6. Unwrap the log and cut it into ¼-inch slices. Put the disks on the baking pan about 1 inch apart.

7. Bake, rotating the pan 180 degrees halfway through the baking time, until the pucks are lightly browned, about 15 minutes.

8. Let the pucks cool completely, still on the pan, on a wire rack.

9. Store the cooled pucks in an airtight container at room temperature. They will keep for up to 1 week.

PORK RILLETTES WITH GREEN PEPPERCORNS

4 CUPS

2 pounds boneless pork shoulder, cut into 1-inch cubes

½ teaspoon ground cloves

½ teaspoon white pepper

½ teaspoon ground ginger

½ teaspoon grated nutmeg

2 teaspoons fine sea salt

2 garlic cloves, peeled

1 bay leaf

⅔ cup (5¼ ounces) dry white wine

1 cup (8 ounces) robust extra-virgin olive oil

2 tablespoons green peppercorns in brine, drained and rinsed

Traditionally this unctuous spread results from slow cooking an equal amount of pork meat and fat. Spread on crusty bread or toast, it pairs well with predinner drinks or serves as a satisfying first course.

This recipe omits the added pork fat and uses a robust extra-virgin olive oil instead, making a slightly lighter but equally delicious version. A meat-loving friend, who thinks nothing of making 100 *confit* duck legs, was amazed by this dish.

The seasonings, *quatre épices*, are a French standby for flavoring meats, and the green peppercorns provide a little zip.

1. Preheat the oven to 250°F.

2. Put the pork cubes in a large bowl. Combine the spices and salt and sprinkle them over the meat. Toss the meat until it is well covered with the spices.

3. Tightly arrange the meat in a casserole so that it fits in one layer. Tuck the garlic cloves and the bay leaf between pieces of meat. Add the wine and olive oil, pushing on the meat to submerge it. Add a little more oil if necessary.

4. Cut a piece of parchment paper the exact size of the casserole. Place it directly on top of the meat. Put a cover on the casserole.

5. Bring the casserole to a simmer on top of the stove, then put it in the oven.

6. Bake until the meat is very tender and separates easily with a fork, about 4 hours. Any fat clinging to the meat will be very soft, but not completely melted.

7. When the meat is cooked, remove the parchment paper and the bay leaf. Put a colander over a large bowl and carefully pour the meat and liquid into the colander. Reserve the liquid. Shred each piece of meat with two forks, transferring it to a bowl as you work. Mix the green peppercorns into the shredded meat. Mix the strained liquid back into the meat. Pack the mixture in crocks for storing. Cover and refrigerate. The rillettes will keep for 1 week in the refrigerator and for 1 month in the freezer.

8. Bring the rillettes to room temperature before serving.

SAFFRON AND FENNEL SEED CRACKERS

ABOUT 30 CRACKERS

¼ teaspoon saffron threads

¾ cup water (6 ounces), divided

¼ cup (2 ounces) medium extra-virgin olive oil

2½ cups (12½ ounces by weight) unbleached all-purpose flour

2 teaspoons fine sea salt

2 tablespoons whole fennel seeds for topping

2 teaspoons fleur de sel for topping

You can't buy crackers this tasty in a store. Eat them alone or top them with spreadable cheese or some of the sauces that can double as spreads (see p. 71–89).

(see p. 71–89)

Saffron threads are the stigmas from the *crocus sativus* flower. Each flower only produces three threads, and they are harvested by hand, making saffron the most expensive spice in the world. Fortunately only a touch is needed—in fact, too much saffron in a dish will give it a bitter, medicinal taste. Even though the threads need to be dried and/or soaked before using to release their intensity, they're a better choice than ground saffron because they will last longer.

1. Heat a small skillet over high heat until a drop of water dances on the surface. Add the saffron and shake the pan until the threads become brittle, about 30 seconds. Scrape the threads into a mortar and grind them to a powder with a pestle. Heat ¼ cup of the water and pour it over the saffron threads. Cool to room temperature.

2. Pour the saffron-infused water, along with the crushed saffron threads, into a medium bowl. Add the remaining ½ cup cool water to the mortar to collect any saffron bits left behind and pour it into the bowl. Add the olive oil.

3. Stir the flour and salt together in a small bowl. Add them to the saffron mixture all at once and stir with a rubber spatula until the water is absorbed. Dribble in a little more water as needed to moisten any flour at the bottom of the bowl. Turn the dough onto a lightly floured work surface and knead about 10 turns, until the dough is smooth. Divide the dough into two balls, flatten them, and cover them with a kitchen towel while the oven heats.

4. Position two racks in the oven and preheat it to 500°F. Line two baking pans with parchment paper.

5. Roll each piece of dough into a rectangle $1/16$ inch thick and roughly 12 by 14 inches. Roll up one rectangle onto a rolling pin and transfer it to a baking sheet. Transfer the other rectangle onto the second baking sheet. Poke the rectangles all over with a fork (use a dough docker if you have one). Cut the dough with a pizza cutter into triangles, squares, or other shapes of your choice. Moisten the dough with a pastry brush dipped in water. Sprinkle the fennel seeds and fleur de sel on top.

6. Bake, rotating the pans 180 degrees halfway through the baking time, until the crackers are well browned, about 15 minutes.

7. Transfer the pans to a rack to cool.

8. Store the crackers in an airtight container at room temperature. They will keep for up to 1 week.

SAVORY LOAF WITH SHEEP CHEESE AND OLIVES

1 LOAF, 8 SLICES

1⅓ cups (6⅔ ounces by weight) unbleached all-purpose flour

1¼ teaspoons baking powder

½ teaspoon fine sea salt

4 extra-large eggs, at room temperature

½ cup (4 ounces) buttermilk, at room temperature

½ cup (4 ounces) medium extra-virgin olive oil, plus more for the pan

4 ounces firm sheep-milk cheese such as Manchego, grated

4 ounces pitted green olives, coarsely chopped

2 teaspoons fresh thyme leaves

freshly ground black pepper

I first encountered loaves that looked like pound cakes but included chunks of ham and cheese instead of being sweet at a market in southwest France. My husband and I bought some to serve with aperitifs for a fish dinner we were cooking with friends at their renovated thirteenth-century house. Back home in San Francisco, I found a similar loaf at Tartine bakery. Then I found Isabel Brancq's delightful book *Cakes et Terrines*, which offers recipes for similar savory loaves. This was inspired by one of her suggestions.

Using the same base of eggs, flour, baking powder, milk, and extra-virgin olive oil, you can vary the taste by using different cheeses, pieces of cooked meat or fish, and spices and herbs. If the mix you choose is not strong-flavored, use a delicate olive oil. Heartier ingredients can stand up to a medium or even a robust olive oil.

Cut into cubes, this loaf is great with aperitifs, or slices of it make a nice first course accompanied by a salad.

1. Position the rack in the middle of the oven and preheat it to 375°F. Oil an 8½-by-4½-inch loaf pan.

2. Sift the flour, baking powder, and salt together into a bowl. Set aside.

3. Whisk the eggs, buttermilk, and olive oil in a medium bowl until well combined.

4. Whisk the dry ingredients into the eggs.

5. Fold in the cheese, olives, and thyme and a few turns of freshly ground pepper.

6. Pour the batter into the baking pan and bake until puffed and browned and a skewer inserted in the center comes out clean, 40 to 45 minutes.

7. Cool the loaf on a rack, then remove from the pan.

SMOKED FISH SPREAD

ABOUT 1½ CUPS

7½ ounces boneless, skinless smoked trout, coarsely chopped

2 scallions, green tops removed, sliced

1 tablespoon chopped parsley

1 tablespoon rinsed, coarsely chopped preserved lemon (see recipe, p. 102)

2 tablespoons (1 ounce) delicate extra-virgin olive oil, plus more if desired

fine sea salt and freshly ground pepper

snipped chives for garnish

This can be prepared almost instantly, if you have preserved lemons on hand. High-quality smoked trout is available at many markets. Take the filets from the package, remove the skin, check for bones, and you're ready to go. Although a medium or robust extra-virgin olive oil should round out the flavor of smoked fish, I think it competes here, so I suggest a delicate oil.

Spread on toasted baguette slices and serve with aperitifs or mound on lettuce and serve as a first course.

1. Put the trout, scallions, parsley, and preserved lemon in the bowl of a food processor. Pulse in short bursts until the fish is shredded. With the machine running, pour the olive oil through the feed tube and process until a coarse but cohesive paste forms. If you prefer a smoother spread, add more oil.

2. Taste for salt and pepper.

3. Use immediately or store in the refrigerator for up to a week. Serve garnished with chives.

TWO-OLIVE TAPENADE

ABOUT 1 CUP

1 cup (4 ounces by weight) pitted green olives, rinsed and patted dry

1 cup (4 ounces by weight) pitted Niçoise-style olives, rinsed and patted dry

1 tablespoon capers, preferably salt-cured, rinsed and patted dry

1 garlic clove, peeled and sliced

2 anchovy filets, either purchased or *crudo* packed in salt, rinsed and patted dry

½ teaspoon whole cumin seeds

freshly ground black pepper

1½ tablespoons (3 ounces) medium extra-virgin olive oil

This Provençal olive spread is usually made with Niçoise-style olives, which are small cured ripe olives, and olive oil made in the same region, which is generally delicate. This recipe uses an equal mix of Niçoise-style olives, such as Coquillo, and green ones. I like it with a medium oil, but use a delicate one if you prefer.

Many stores now sell olives in bulk, and that is a good source for this recipe. Buy them in a store with a high turnover so the olives are fresh. I have found both green and Niçoise olives that are pitted, which makes this easy to prepare.

If you have cured anchovies according to the recipe on page 123, use them. Otherwise, use filets packed in olive oil.

This is delicious served on slices of toasted baguette, plus it is very versatile. Mix a dollop into deviled egg filling, spread it on sandwiches, or stuff a few tablespoons under the skin of a chicken before roasting.

1. Put the olives, capers, garlic, anchovies, cumin seeds, and several grinds of pepper in the bowl of a food processor. Pulse in short bursts until everything is finely chopped. It should not be a paste. With the machine running, add the olive oil.

2. Use immediately or store in the refrigerator for up to a week.

ASCOLI-STYLE FRIED OLIVES

4 SERVINGS

20 large green stuffed olives, drained and carefully dried

½ cup unbleached all-purpose flour

1 large egg, beaten

½ cup semolina flour

about 1 cup (8 ounces) delicate extra-virgin olive oil

While vacationing in Italy's Marche region in the fall of 2006, my husband and I visited Ascoli Piceno, a jewel of a town not far from the Adriatic Sea. Large green olives, pitted, then stuffed with a meat mixture, battered, and fried, are a specialty. We ate them in a restaurant, at a nearby *agriturismo* (farmhouse resort), and as part of a picnic lunch. A quick cooking heats them through but retains their crunch.

Back home, I followed the recipe in a cookbook I bought while in Italy. The olives were delicious, but the pitting and the stuffing took time. This is my version using olives that are already pitted and stuffed. Choose a stuffing that you like, be it garlic, almonds, or cheese. If you buy olives at one of the olive bars that are now in many stores, make sure they are fresh. Alternatively, buy olives in a jar.

These olives are fried in extra-virgin olive oil. The oil will not smoke if it is heated to 350 degrees Fahrenheit, a good temperature to use for this recipe. Choose an oil with a delicate flavor; certainly not your most expensive bottle!

Serve with aperitifs or as part of a salad for a first course.

1. Preheat the oven to 150°F.

2. Arrange three bowls on a work surface. Put the flour in one, the egg in the second, and the semolina in the third.

3. Working with a few olives at a time, roll them to coat them with the flour. Dip them in the egg, removing them with a fork and tapping them on the side of the bowl to remove excess egg. Finally, roll them in semolina. Put the coated olives on a plate.

4. Place a large plate covered with paper towels in a slightly warmed oven.

5. Put the extra-virgin olive oil in a small pan that can withstand high heat. There should be enough oil to submerge four olives at a time. Add more if needed.

6. Set a deep-frying thermometer in the pan and heat the oil to 350°F. Fry the olives in batches of four, cooking them until they are golden brown, about 3 minutes. Use a slotted spoon to transfer them to the plate in the oven.

7. Serve hot.

APOLLO OLIVE OIL

PO Box 1054
Oregon House, California 95962
530 692 9132
www.apollooliveoil.com

I didn't know from one day to the next when Apollo would be pressing olives, and I wanted to see their special mill at work. "Call me Tuesday morning," Pablo Voitzuk, the sales manager, said. I did. Pablo called Gianni Stefanini, the miller, and returned my call. "You're in luck. I'll meet you at four-thirty this afternoon and take you to the winery where we're working," Pablo said.

I followed Pablo to the winery's gated entrance. We ascended to the building along paved roads, through roundabouts with gold statues in the middle and extensive landscaping, a striking contrast to the rural setting. (Oregon House is a hamlet in the Sierra Foothills southeast of Oroville. A general store/gas station at a crossroad seems to be the hub of the community.) Curiously, the terraced hillsides looked bare. At the top of a hill, we drove to the back of a large winery building that looked as if construction had been halted some time ago. An Apollo Olive Oil sign was tacked to the top of a door on the

left side, and this inconspicuous entrance led to a special vacuum milling operation, one of four in the world, and the only one in this country. When Gianni and Steven Dambeck, a fellow owner, wanted to change their method from the traditional stone mill to something more modern, their friend Darrell Corti, the chairman of the Los Angeles International Olive Oil competition, sent them to Marco Mugelli, an Italian olive oil expert who had been experimenting with vacuum pressing for about twelve years. During standard milling operations, the olive paste is exposed to oxygen, which decreases the healthy polyphenols in the oil. Marco's goal is to eliminate as much oxygen as possible. To that end, he has developed vacuum-sealed malaxation tanks and a centrifugal decanter that forms a seal as it spins. Apollo acquired one of his presses in 2005.

Marco's thoughts about milling start with the timing of the harvest. He advocates monitoring the Brix (sugar percentage) of the fruit, waiting for just the right moment when the sugar level goes down and the oil level rises. And because the olives start to decompose the minute they leave the tree, they should be pressed as soon as possible. Marco is always pushing the Apollo crew to shorten that time. Now it is no more than four hours.

Pablo handed me earplugs and we stepped inside. The shrill whine of the machinery differed from the throaty sounds of other mills. Gianni, wearing ear protectors, sat at a computer screen that monitored the action of the four malaxation tanks. A picture of Apollo and two gold medal certificates from the Los Angeles competition hung on a wall next to him. Because the paste is under vacuum, he can leave it in the malaxers as long as he deems necessary, sometimes up to an hour. Unlike most other operations, the oil is filtered immediately as it leaves the decanter to remove particles that might lead to its degradation.

All this effort has paid off. Apollo has produced batches of extra-virgin olive oil with 700 parts per million of polyphenols. Conventional oils may contain 150 to 250 ppm; the Apollo Barouni oil pressed in 2006 contained just under 400 ppm. This means a healthier oil and one that will last longer. According to Gianni, Marco sees a change in the philosophy of oil production. Polyphenol content was never a goal of millers in the past; now Gianni knows several who deem it important. In ten years, Marco predicts that the polyphenol content of some oils may be up to 1,000 ppm.

Gianni handed his ear protectors to an assistant, and we went outside to a picnic table, snacking on Pablo's home-cured olives as we talked. They had started milling at one P.M. and, after pressing about five tons of olives, would finish about three A.M. The stone mill took much longer because the process is slower and the stones must be shut down to transfer the paste to the malaxation tanks.

The milling lasts for forty days; during half of those days, when there are more olives to process, the mill runs twenty hours at a time, in two ten-hour shifts. Each olive variety (they have forty-four) is milled separately. Then, when the press is shut down for the season, Edward Schulten, master blender, guides the millers in developing oils with distinct characteristics.

As darkness set in, Gianni reminisced about his grandmother giving him olive oil as a child. At the first sign of any illness, she insisted that he swallow a tablespoon before breakfast and continue daily until he was well again—and this was oil with normal antioxidant properties. His grandmother would have appreciated the super-polyphenol oil.

McEVOY RANCH OLIVE OIL

5935 Red Hill Road
Petaluma, California 94953
707 778 2307
www.mcevoyranch.com

Nan McEvoy didn't know anything about growing olives in 1990, when she bought her 550-acre ranch in the west Marin hills north of San Francisco. The land, zoned for agricultural use, was once a dairy farm, but Nan didn't want cows. Because she frequently made trips to Italy and always brought home olive oil, she thought of planting olives. County officials discouraged the notion; they didn't think the climate was right. But Nan persevered. She met Maurizio Castelli, a Tuscan olive and wine expert, through Maggie Blyth Klein, author and co-owner of Oliveto restaurant in Oakland. He was optimistic about her plan. Encouraged by his advice, the newspaper heiress (Michael DeYoung, her grandfather, founded the *San Francisco Chronicle* in 1865) imported her first batch of a thousand trees in 1991. US Agricultural inspectors laboriously examined each immigrant bare-root tree upon arrival, taking their time. Some trees were returned to the incorrect boxes, so many were

misidentified when they arrived at the ranch. The next shipment was two thousand trees. They were Tuscan varietials—Frantoio, Leccino, Pendolino, Maurino, Leccio del Corno—except one, Coratina, which is from Puglia. Propagations from these originals increased the orchard over the years; now there are eighteen thousand trees total.

Trees are propagated on the ranch in a nursery that was once one of the dairy barns. Rather than being planted, they are for sale. The loft space has been removed to let light in through the tall roof. To start the propagation, workers cut branches from existing trees, then remove smaller branches from these. The leaves are stripped from the bottom, leaving only a few on top. The tiny trees-to-be are put in a perlite mixture and set on special tables, each heated from underneath and enclosed in a mini greenhouse made from heavy plastic on wooden supports. Once the trees start to develop roots, they are moved to four-inch pots that contain a sterile mix of perlite, peat moss, and vermiculite. When the roots become more established and the trees are about six inches tall, they are moved again, this time into one-gallon pots. They continue to grow and are sold either in these pots when they are about one and a half years old, or moved to larger pots to further mature. Along with the Italian varietals, the nursery has trees with other pedigrees for sale. Samantha Kerby, the nursery manager, has a few that are cuttings from the University of California at Davis. All are from the Middle East, with names like Chalkioki, Hamid, Giarffa, and Menara. She wants to espalier them so they intertwine, a project she calls her five-year Middle East peace plan.

In addition to selecting trees for the ranch, Maurizio Castelli also helped choose equipment for the mill. There is a stone mill as well as a disc mill. In addition to the usual horizontal decanter, he chose the selective filtration apparatus known as Sinolea processing. Since no pressure is applied to the paste, this method produces free-run oil of very high quality. But it is a complicated system that requires high maintenance. McEvoy has the only Sinolea processor in the country.

Organic management and careful agricultural practices are important priorities. Spent pomace is composted with manure from nearby farms and applied to the orchard; cover crops are planted to enrich the soil, and sheep instead of mowers control weeds; rainwater is collected in ponds and used for irrigation. Trees from the nursery and other products, such as jams made from fruit grown on the ranch, are all organic. To date, McEvoy is the largest producer of organic estate-grown olive oil in the country.

SAUCES

The pestos in this chapter are naturals for dressing pastas, but they have other uses too. Try the wild arugula and cilantro pestos, as well as the Muhammara and Romesco sauces as dips. Extra-virgin olive oil is what makes these offerings so tasty.

A Trio of Pestos

The word *pesto* means "pounded" in Italian, and these sauces are traditionally made in a mortar and pestle. The notion of pounded condiments dates back to Roman days, and the practice is quite old in the Middle East. Although purists might disagree, using a processor is a good way to make these sauces and is certainly less time-consuming. Adding the greens in two batches prevents overprocessing.

CILANTRO PESTO

ABOUT ¾ CUP

2 cups tightly packed cilantro leaves, divided

¼ teaspoon fine sea salt

freshly ground black pepper

6 tablespoons (3 ounces) medium extra-virgin olive oil, divided

2 teaspoons Persian lime olive oil

A little Persian lime olive oil adds another flavor dimension to this pesto. Use it as a dressing for a salad of avocados, tomatoes, and onions, as a dip for raw vegetables, or drizzle a little on feta cheese and serve it on crackers with aperitifs. The medium extra-virgin olive oil adds a little zip.

1. Put about half the cilantro leaves, the salt, and a few grindings of pepper in the small bowl of a food processor. With the motor running, drizzle about half the extra-virgin olive oil through the feed tube, stopping occasionally to scrape the bowl. Add the rest of the cilantro and, with the motor running, drizzle in the rest of the extra-virgin olive oil, then the Persian lime olive oil. Correct the seasoning.

2. If not using immediately, transfer the sauce to a bowl, cover it with plastic wrap placed directly on top of the sauce, and refrigerate. It will keep for a week.

BASIL PESTO

ABOUT ¾ CUP, ENOUGH FOR 1 POUND OF PASTA

2 cups tightly packed basil leaves (1 large bunch), divided

2 garlic cloves, peeled and coarsely chopped

2 tablespoons (1 ounce by weight) pine nuts

¼ teaspoon fine sea salt

¼ cup (1 ounce by weight) grated Parmigiano Reggiano

¼ cup (2 ounces) medium extra-virgin olive oil, divided

There are many opinions about how to make this sauce—the size of the basil leaves, which cheese to use and how much, the amount of olive oil, whether a touch of butter is appropriate, or whether the consistency should be pastelike or a suspension of the components in the oil. All are open to debate. I will add the style of olive oil to the list. In Liguria, the home of this sauce, a mild, buttery olive oil is usually the choice. But with the heady aroma of the basil and the bits of raw garlic, I prefer a medium extra-virgin olive oil.

Choose the pine nuts carefully, tasting one before buying if possible to be sure that they aren't rancid, a common problem.

The classic way to serve pesto is with a pasta such as linguini. A drizzle of pasta-cooking water while tossing the pasta helps the sauce coat every strand. A dollop of pesto will also enliven a hearty soup, such as minestrone.

1. Put about half the basil, the garlic, the pine nuts, the salt, and about half of the cheese in the small bowl of a food processor. With the processor running, drizzle about half of the olive oil through the feed tube. Scrape down the bowl. Add the remaining basil and cheese. With the processor running, add the rest of the oil. Process until the paste just comes together; don't over-process. Correct the seasoning.

2. If not using immediately, transfer the sauce to a bowl, cover it with plastic wrap placed directly on top of the sauce, and refrigerate. It will keep for a week.

WILD ARUGULA PESTO

ABOUT ¾ CUP

2 cups tightly packed arugula
leaves, divided

¼ teaspoon fine sea salt

½ cup (4 ounces) delicate
extra-virgin olive oil, divided

A friend warned me. She planted wild arugula in her garden—it went to seed and now pops up everywhere. But I love the peppery taste of this variety, more gutsy than its tamer cousin, so I planted it too. I try to keep it contained by removing the flowers before they go to seed, but I still have a few volunteer plants in unexpected places in my garden. Wild arugula is sometimes available at farmers' markets and in produce stores; if you can't find it, use the tamer variety.

This isn't a classic pesto, with garlic, cheese, and nuts—there are only three ingredients: the greens, oil, and salt. The sauce retains a vibrant color, maybe because of the chlorophyll in the leaves and the polyphenols in the oil. Use it to dress pasta or spread it on toasted slices of baguette and serve as an appetizer.

A buttery, delicate extra-virgin olive oil, or even one with some tropical notes, will tame the spicy leaves.

1. Put about half the arugula leaves and the salt in the small bowl of a food processor. With the motor running, drizzle about half the olive oil through the feed tube, stopping occasionally to scrape the bowl. Add the rest of the arugula and, with the motor running, drizzle in the rest of the olive oil. Correct the seasoning.

2. If not using immediately, transfer the sauce to a bowl, cover it with plastic wrap placed directly on top of the sauce, and refrigerate. It will keep for a week.

A Family of Vinaigrettes

Many salads can be dressed by merely tossing them with extra-virgin olive oil and something acidic like lemon juice, but other salads benefit from an emulsified dressing to thoroughly coat the ingredients. Vinaigrettes let you mix and match the oil and acids and allow for added flavors such as mustard or cheese.

To test the vinaigrette for seasoning, dip a leaf of lettuce (or a morsel of whatever you are dressing) through it, then taste the lettuce. This will give a more accurate appraisal than sampling the vinaigrette alone.

Use vinegars with an acidity of 6 percent, which is indicated on the bottle. The exception is sherry vinegar, which is more acidic, often as high as 7.5 percent.

BLUE CHEESE VINAIGRETTE

⅓ CUP, ENOUGH TO DRESS A SALAD FOR 4

about 1 tablespoon (½ ounce by weight) blue cheese

1 tablespoon (½ ounce) white wine vinegar

¼ teaspoon fine sea salt

freshly ground black pepper

4 tablespoons (2 ounces) delicate extra-virgin olive oil, divided

2 teaspoons water

Try this with sliced pears or apples; the sweetness of the fruit cuts the earthy sharpness of the cheese. Sprinkle the top of the fruit with raisins or chopped toasted pecans. This dressing would also enliven a salad of romaine hearts. Use your favorite blue cheese, one that is not too salty. A delicate extra-virgin olive oil balances the cheese.

1. Put the cheese and vinegar in a small deep bowl, coffee mug, or a 1-cup measure and mash with a fork to make a paste, leaving a few lumps of cheese whole. Add the salt and pepper. Slowly pour 2 tablespoons of the extra-virgin olive oil into the bowl, beating constantly with the fork. Beat in the water, then the remaining 2 tablespoons of extra-virgin olive oil. Taste for seasoning.

MUSTARD VINAIGRETTE

¹/₃ CUP, ENOUGH TO DRESS A SALAD FOR 4

2 teaspoons red wine vinegar

¹/₄ teaspoon fine sea salt

freshly ground black pepper

about ¹/₄ teaspoon strong Dijon mustard

4 tablespoons (2 ounces) medium or robust extra-virgin olive oil, divided

2 teaspoons water

Tucked into the southeast corner of the Place de la Madeleine in Paris stands a Maille mustard store. Although a plethora of mustards is available, the most exciting feature of the store for a mustard aficionado is the display of three pumps, similar to those found in bars to draw beer, in the middle of the counter toward the front of the store. Here mustard is available *en pression*; it splutters from the pump in fits and starts into an earthenware crock. If a customer arrives with an empty Maille crock, it will be filled for a fraction of the price of a new one. This fresh mustard has a zing and brightness that is lacking in jars found here, even if they are imported. If you aren't fortunate enough to have a fresh supply from the store, use a tangy Dijon-style mustard.

Mustard's emulsifying ability binds the oil and vinegar in this vinaigrette. This goes well with the Gruyère Salad (see p. 98) or any other salad when a hint of mustard is welcome, such as a Niçoise or a chicken salad.

1. Put the vinegar, the salt, and a few grindings of pepper into a small deep bowl, a coffee mug, or a 1-cup measure. Take some mustard from the jar on the tines of a fork and beat it into the vinegar. Slowly pour 2 tablespoons of the extra-virgin olive oil into the bowl, beating constantly with the fork. Beat in the water, then the remaining 2 tablespoons of extra-virgin olive oil. Taste for seasoning.

SHERRY VINAIGRETTE WITH SHALLOTS

⅓ CUP, ENOUGH TO DRESS A SALAD FOR 4

2 teaspoons minced shallots

1 tablespoon (½ ounce) sherry vinegar

¼ teaspoon fine sea salt

freshly ground black pepper

4 tablespoons (2 ounces) medium extra-virgin olive oil, divided

2 teaspoons water

Sherry vinegar, with its sweet-sour taste, is reminiscent of balsamic vinegar but not as complex (or as expensive). Use this to dress a salad of hearty greens or toss it with cooked greens such as kale. It's a good dressing for the Quinoa Salad on page 101, but because that salad contains scallions, omit the shallots in the vinaigrette.

1. Put the shallots, vinegar, salt, and a few grindings of pepper into a small deep bowl, a coffee mug, or a 1-cup measure. Slowly pour 2 tablespoons of the extra-virgin olive oil into the bowl, beating constantly with the fork. Beat in the water, then the remaining 2 tablespoons of extra-virgin olive oil. Taste for seasoning.

CREAMY VINAIGRETTE

²/₃ CUP

1 extra-large egg yolk, at room temperature

3 tablespoons (1½ ounces) heavy whipping cream, at room temperature

1 recipe Mustard Vinaigrette (see p. 78) made using a delicate extra-virgin olive oil

2 teaspoons lemon juice, more to taste

1 tablespoon chopped fresh tarragon

1 tablespoon snipped chives

I remember being served a sauce like this in a simple country restaurant on a trip to France many years ago. After a rustic main dish, the wife of the chef brought a glass bowl piled high with whole leaves of tender butter lettuce. She poured a creamy sauce over them and gently tossed the salad, then left the bowl on the table so we could serve ourselves. The dressing bathed each leaf, and the wisp of tarragon enlivened the taste.

In addition to dressing salads, you could also nap slices of cold chicken or poached salmon with this sauce, or even use it as a dip for artichokes.

1. Put the egg yolk in the small bowl of a food processor. With the machine running, drizzle the whipping cream through the feed tube. Next, drizzle the vinaigrette into the bowl. Add the lemon juice. Correct the seasoning. Add the herbs and pulse a few times to mix them into the vinaigrette.

Olive Oil Mayonnaise with Variations

In his book, *Food and Cooking*, Harold McGee reports that mayonnaise with olive oil as its only fat is not always stable because it contains mono- and diglycerides, which interfere with the emulsifiers in the egg yolk. It may make a perfect emulsion at first, but after an hour or two, oil drops may coalesce and separate. However, I have not had a problem with this recipe that uses extra-virgin olive oil; it has maintained a perfect emulsion for at least three days in the refrigerator.

Although purists hand whisk the eggs and oil to make an emulsion, using a food processor, as well as two egg yolks instead of one, is faster and more foolproof. This method can produce a thicker sauce. If the consistency is not to your liking, add a little more water at the end.

Use a delicate extra-virgin olive oil for an all-purpose mayonnaise. The spicier spreads can take a more robust oil.

ALL-PURPOSE MAYONNAISE

ABOUT 1¼ CUPS

2 extra-large egg yolks, at room temperature

1 tablespoon (½ ounce) lemon juice, more to taste

¼ teaspoon fine sea salt

freshly ground black pepper

1 cup (8 ounces) delicate extra-virgin olive oil

1 tablespoon (½ ounce) cool water

My husband loves mayonnaise. He puts it on sandwiches of every description, slathering each slice of bread until the crumb is invisible. Recently he bought a jar of his favorite brand only to discover that the taste had changed radically. A glance at the ingredient list told the story. In an effort to make it cholesterol free (it already contained only a minute amount) and less caloric, the new formula contained more water than oil and a slew of what could only be called food additives. He threw it away in disgust, vowing that we will make all future mayonnaise consumed at our house.

1. Put the egg yolks, lemon juice, salt, and 4 grindings of pepper in the small bowl of a food processor.

2. With the machine running, drizzle the extra-virgin olive oil through the feed tube, starting with a few drops at a time and gradually increasing to a thin stream. Make sure all the oil is emulsified, not floating on top, before adding more. The sound will change to a splat as the mayonnaise thickens. Add all the oil, then add the water.

3. If you are not using the mayonnaise immediately, transfer it to a small covered container. It will keep for 3 days in the refrigerator.

AÏOLI

ABOUT 1¼ CUPS

2 garlic cloves, peeled and minced

2 extra-large egg yolks, at room temperature

1 tablespoon (½ ounce) lemon juice, more to taste

¼ teaspoon fine sea salt

freshly ground black pepper

1 cup (8 ounces) medium extra-virgin olive oil

1 tablespoon (½ ounce) cool water

Aïoli is mayonnaise made with fresh garlic, and this addition gives the spread more backbone. It is traditionally served with Provençal fish stews but is equally good on potatoes, especially French fries, and grilled vegetables.

1. Put the garlic, egg yolks, lemon juice, salt, and 4 grindings of pepper in a small bowl of a food processor.

2. With the machine running, drizzle the extra-virgin olive oil through the feed tube, starting with a few drops at a time and gradually increasing to a thin stream. Make sure all the oil is emulsified, not floating on top, before adding more. The sound will change to a splat as the mayonnaise thickens. After adding about a third of the oil, stop the processor and scrape down the sides to make sure that the garlic is being incorporated. Add the remaining oil, then the water. Stop the machine and taste for acidity and salt, adding more if necessary.

3. If you are not using the aïoli immediately, transfer it to a small covered container. It will keep for 3 days in the refrigerator.

CURRY MAYONNAISE

ABOUT 1¼ CUPS

2 extra-large egg yolks, at room temperature

1 tablespoon curry powder (your favorite)

2 tablespoons (1 ounce) cool water, divided

1 tablespoon (½ ounce) lemon juice, more to taste

¼ teaspoon fine sea salt

freshly ground black pepper

1 cup (8 ounces) medium or robust extra-virgin olive oil

I first had French fries with curry mayonnaise at a roadside stand outside Brussels. The Belgians love their fries and almost always dip them in mayonnaise. Although the practice may seem excessive, it's a great combination.

Use this instead of regular mayonnaise to make deviled eggs or for pork sandwiches. I like to steam mussels and serve them on the half shell at room temperature with a squiggle of curry mayonnaise on top.

1. Break up the egg yolks with a fork in a small bowl then beat in the curry powder, 1 tablespoon of the water, the lemon juice, salt, and 4 grindings of pepper. Transfer this slurry to the small bowl of a processor.

2. With the machine running, drizzle the extra-virgin olive oil through the feed tube, starting with a few drops at a time and gradually increasing to a thin stream. Make sure all the oil is emulsified, not floating on top, before adding more. The sound will change to a splat as the mayonnaise thickens. Add all the oil, then the other tablespoon of water.

3. If you are not using the mayonnaise immediately, transfer it to a small covered container. It will keep for 3 days in the refrigerator.

GREEN SAUCE

1 CUP

1 cup packed flat-leaf parsley
  leaves

1 tablespoon fresh thyme leaves

2 garlic cloves, peeled and finely
  chopped

2 scallions, green tops removed,
  thinly sliced

1/2 teaspoon fine sea salt

freshly ground black pepper

1/8 teaspoon ground cayenne
  pepper

1/4 cup (2 ounces) red wine
  vinegar

1/2 cup (4 ounces) robust
  extra-virgin olive oil

This sauce is almost a vegetable course on its own and is a particularly good match for grilled meat or vegetables. It will enliven meat sandwiches or even poached eggs.

Parsley is the main greenery, but mix and match other herbs to your taste. Because this sauce contains garlic and cayenne pepper, use a robust extra-virgin olive oil.

1. Put the parsley, thyme, garlic, scallions, salt, a few turns of black pepper, the cayenne pepper, and vinegar in the small bowl of a food processor.

2. With the machine running, drizzle the extra-virgin olive oil through the feed tube, stopping once to scrape down the sides of the bowl. Process until the herbs are finely chopped and the sauce is slightly emulsified.

MUHAMMARA

1 GENEROUS CUP

3/4 cup (3 ounces by weight)
   walnut pieces

2 medium red bell peppers

5 tablespoons (2 1/2 ounces)
   robust extra-virgin olive oil

1/2 cup fresh bread crumbs

1 garlic clove, peeled and sliced

1 tablespoon (1/2 ounce)
   lemon juice

1 teaspoon pomegranate
   molasses

1 teaspoon fine sea salt

1/2 teaspoon dried Aleppo pepper

This is truly an all-purpose sauce, best made with a robust oil. Aleppo, Syria, is the home of muhammara, although it is made throughout Syria and in southern Turkey. Serve it with pork chops or tuna steaks, slather it on bread when making hearty sandwiches, or serve it as a spread on Saffron and Fennel Seed Crackers (see recipe, p. 59).

If you have any Scallion and Rosemary Focaccia (see recipe, p. 166) on hand, use it to make the bread crumbs.

1. To toast the walnuts, preheat the oven to 350°F. Arrange the walnuts in a single layer in a small pan and roast until you can just detect their aroma and they are lightly browned, about 5 minutes. Cool to room temperature. (This can be done ahead.)

2. Roast the bell peppers over a gas flame or on a charcoal grill until they are black all over. Slip them into a paper bag and let them cool. Peel off the skin, cut them in half, and remove the seeds and ribs. Chop the peppers coarsely.

3. Heat 1 tablespoon of the extra-virgin olive oil in a small skillet over high heat until it trembles, becomes aromatic, and a drop of water sputters when it hits the oil. Add the bread crumbs and cook, stirring frequently with a wooden spoon, until they are lightly browned and crisp, about 2 minutes.

4. Put the walnuts, peppers, bread crumbs, garlic, lemon juice, pomegranate molasses, salt, and Aleppo pepper in the bowl of a processor.

5. With the machine running, drizzle the remaining olive oil into the processor to make a thick sauce.

6. If you are not using the muhammara immediately, transfer it to a small covered container. The sauce will keep in the refrigerator for about 1 week. Return to room temperature before serving.

ROMESCO SAUCE

1 GENEROUS CUP

½ cup (2½ ounces by weight) blanched almonds

2 medium red bell peppers

½ teaspoon fine sea salt, plus additional to taste

3 garlic cloves, peeled and sliced

¼ teaspoon hot *pimentón* paprika

¼ cup (2 ounces) robust extra-virgin olive oil

2 teaspoons red wine vinegar

fine sea salt

freshly ground black pepper

Romesco means three things in Catalonia, its birthplace. It is a type of dried pepper (also called *nyora*), a seafood dish, and a sauce that typically contains ground almonds or hazelnuts, dried *nyora* peppers, and tomatoes.

Since the specific peppers are not available here, I have substituted *pimentón* pepper. *Pimentón* peppers are grown in the northwest of Spain and are carefully dried over oak fires before they are stemmed, seeded, and reduced to a fine powder, or paprika. Depending on the peppers, the resulting spice can be mild (*dulce*), medium (*agridulce*), or hot (*picante*). It is available in some grocery stores or online. I have omitted the tomatoes, so the sauce can be made year-round, not just at the height of the tomato season.

In Catalonia it is probably made with a delicate oil such as Arbequina, but a robust oil goes well with the garlic and dried pepper.

This sauce is wonderful on grilled sardines or other fish with a distinct flavor. It also makes a lively topping for grilled vegetables, a dip for raw vegetables, or an instant appetizer when spread on a cracker.

1. To toast the almonds, preheat the oven to 350°F. Arrange the almonds in a single layer in a small pan and roast until you can just detect their aroma and they are lightly browned, about 5 minutes. Let them cool to room temperature. (This can be done ahead.)

2. Roast the bell peppers over a gas flame or on a charcoal grill until they are black all over. Slip them into a paper bag and let them cool. Peel off the skin, cut them in half, and remove the seeds and ribs. Chop the peppers coarsely.

3. Put the almonds in a food processor and pulse until they are fine, but not a powder. They need not be uniform; some larger pieces will add texture to the sauce.

4. Add the peppers, salt, garlic, and *pimentón*. Process to a thick, coarse paste. The sauce should have discernible pieces of almonds and visible flecks of red pepper.

5. With the machine running, drizzle in the extra-virgin olive oil, then add the vinegar. Check the seasoning.

6. If you are not using the sauce immediately, transfer the sauce to a small covered container. It will keep in the refrigerator for about 1 week. Return to room temperature before serving.

SAVOR
OLIVE OIL

San Antonio Valley Olive Ranch
53850 Bradley-Lockwood Rd.
Bradley, California 93426
805 472 2780
www.savoroliveoil.com

It wasn't easy to find San Antonio Valley Olive Ranch. I wanted to talk to Maria Weinerth about the oil that won the best of show medal in the delicate domestic class at the 2007 Los Angeles competition—an Arbequina oil that had quickly sold out. Google searches led me to other Savor Olive Oil sites, but not to Maria Weinerth. Journalist Olivia Wu, who covered the competition, helped me with the lead I needed.

It was close to 100 degrees when I pulled into Maria's driveway, thirty-five miles north of Paso Robles. A cheery woman with long, flowing hair, she greeted me at the door and led me into a pleasantly cool room protected from the sun by overhanging eaves on all sides.

I knew she was passionate about olives when she told me of her plans to send pits of some of her olives to Europe to determine the variety. The trees were sold to her as Mission, a sort of catchall term for the trees that were brought to the California missions, but she sus-

pects that they are really Manzanillo. They are the majority of the trees planted on the six and a half acres devoted to olives that surround the house. The 360 Arbequina trees that produced the winning oil grow on the enclosure that housed breeder sheep her children raised before they left for college.

The trees are conventionally spaced. "No one here has the machinery to harvest the densely-planted trees," she said. She hires a foreman with a crew to hand-harvest all the olives, but she harvests too—and watches them. "If an olive drops on the ground, I won't let them pick it up," she said. In a good year, the total yield is ten tons. The olives are driven for pressing to mills either in Hollister to the north or Templeton to the south.

Maria and her husband bought the property in 1989 as a weekend getaway while they lived in San Jose. Because she has horses, first they farmed hay. Eventually they built the house and moved. Many of the neighbors grow grapes, but she "didn't want to supply grapes for Two-Buck Chuck" (the nickname for a popular wine sold at the Trader Joe's grocery chain). For her, olives were a logical choice. She grew up in a family with Portuguese heritage that "lived and breathed" olives. Her grandmother, the good cook in the family, used olive oil freely. Plus, the olive trees don't die off the way vines do. "I just love my trees," she told me.

Most of the Mission and Barouni olives go to a mill, but she also sends some to a packer in Visalia who salt cures them, then returns them to her. In addition, she cures her own personal batch. Maria got a five-gallon jug from the refrigerator and removed a few for me to taste. They were tangy and crisp.

Although others bottle the oil and cure the olives, she affixes the labels at home. She sells the oil and cured olives at two farmers' markets and to a few stores that contact her; there is no distributor, no public relations person. "I do everything," she said.

PASOLIVO OLIVE OIL

8530 Vineyard Dr.
Paso Robles, California 93446
805 227 0186
www.pasolivo.com

In the early 1990s, Karen Guth and her then-husband bought a ranch in Paso Robles, situated halfway between Los Angeles and San Francisco, as a weekend getaway from their home in Newport Beach. Karen had never liked living in Southern California, so after she and her husband divorced, she moved to the ranch full time and pondered how best to use the property. It had been a Mennonite dairy farm in the late 1800s. Butter and milk from the farm were transported to the coast and shipped to Los Angeles and San Francisco. An old red barn dating from the early 1900s still stands across from the tasting room. Perhaps thinking of the ranch's history, she bought twelve cows, not dairy animals but Angus, plus a bull. When they reproduced, she sold the offspring. But the cattle were more trouble than dogs. "They were like large pets," she told me. She knew the cattle experiment wouldn't last for long.

Then, like so many other people whose lives are transformed by trips to Europe, she went to Tuscany and was struck by the similarity of a view from a vineyard and the view from her hilltop house. Not wanting to grow grapes, the burgeoning nouveau crop around Paso Robles, she settled on olives.

She signed up for an olive oil production course given by Paul Vossen at the University of California Extension. What she learned gave her confidence to proceed with her plan. She bought her first trees, eight hundred Mission with some pollinizers, in 1996. Next she bought trees from Ridgely Evers, who was planting Tuscan varietals north of San Francisco. Later, more trees came from the McEvoy ranch, also north of San Francisco.

In a quest to learn more, she took a course in the sensory evaluation of olive oil given by the University of California Extension and eventually joined the COOC taste panel.

Karen led me from the living room to the deck to show me the view of almost forty-five acres planted in mostly Tuscan trees. (The original Mission and Manzanillo olives go into her California blend.) The Tuscan olives are picked and milled together; the only single variety milled alone is a Kalamata oil, somewhat of a rarity in California. Customers at the store gravitate to the Tuscan oils more and more, asking for the "strong stuff." It's not only the customers; the Tuscan blend won a best of show in the domestic robust category at the 2007 Los Angeles competition.

Pasolivo also makes citrus oils from their California blend and distilled oils from citrus fruit, either Meyer lemons, limes, or tangerines, which are put into the malaxation tanks with the olive paste. In 2007, the tangerine oil won a best of show medal at the Los Angeles competition.

Karen's son and daughter-in-law work in the business with her, although both she and her son have kept their day jobs as financial analysts. Her son is also the miller. Two years ago they bought a Pieralisi hammer mill and installed it in their small production site behind the tasting room. They press for about two weeks, sometimes running the mill twenty-four hours at a time. Although the press is sophisticated, the rest of the operation is humble—bottles are filled four at a time and labels are hand applied.

They sell everything that they make quite quickly and often have debates about increasing production, but in the short term, that would necessitate buying olives elsewhere or even buying bulk oil. Karen is wary. "I would have a harder time selling oil that wasn't completely ours."

SALADS
AND SOUPS

The recipes in this chapter let the nuances of the olive oils shine because they are such an integral part of the dishes. A salad wouldn't be a salad without dressing, and the oils drizzled on the soups just before serving make their tastes more complex.

FRESH CORN SALAD WITH MINT

6 SERVINGS

6 ears white corn

½ medium-sized sweet onion, peeled and finely chopped

3 stalks celery, thinly sliced

12 fresh peppermint leaves, stacked, rolled, and thinly sliced

1 medium vine-ripened tomato, diced

¼ cup (2 ounces) medium extra-virgin olive oil

1 tablespoon (½ ounce) fresh lemon juice

fleur de sel and freshly ground black pepper

Some years ago, in a moment of unbridled optimism, I planted corn in my San Francisco garden. The plants were indifferent to the sunny southern exposure and warm microclimate—they failed to thrive. So I continue to buy corn instead of growing it myself. In July and August, I buy it at the Anderson Valley Farm Supply at every opportunity.

Dave Gowan, the former owner of the Farm Supply, recently sold his business, but I'm hoping that he won't be able to resist the urge to plant at least a few rows of Silver Queen—a sweet corn, not one of the supersweet hybrids— and sell them at the Farm Supply. It is some of the best corn I have ever had.

I think a medium extra-virgin olive oil is a nice contrast with the sweetness of the corn, but if you want to accentuate the corn's sweetness, use a delicate oil.

1. Bring a large pot of water to a boil. Shuck the corn and remove the silky strands.

2. Put the corn in the pot and return to a boil over high heat. Remove the ears and let them cool.

3. Stand each ear large end down in a large bowl and cut off the kernels, scraping any white liquid from the cobs into the bowl.

4. Add the onion, celery, peppermint, and tomato and mix together.

5. Drizzle the extra-virgin olive oil over the salad and mix again.

6. Sprinkle the lemon juice on top and toss.

7. Season with fleur de sel and pepper and serve.

FUYU PERSIMMON AND FENNEL SALAD

4 SERVINGS

1 small fennel bulb

2 medium Fuyu persimmons, unpeeled

2 scallions, green tops removed, thinly sliced

3 to 4 tablespoons (1½ to 2 ounces) Persian lime olive oil

1 tablespoon (½ ounce) fresh lime juice

fleur de sel and freshly ground black pepper

Fuyu persimmons are the squat variety that are firm when ready to eat. (Their Hachiya cousins are slightly larger with a pointed bottom and must be very soft when eaten to avoid a mouth-puckering astringency.)

A mandoline is the best tool to cut the persimmons and fennel into the very thin slices needed for this salad.

The Persian lime olive oil and lime juice add a refreshing note.

1. Slice the fennel bulb into 1/16-inch slices on a mandoline. Discard the first few slices that contain a large portion of the core.

2. Slice the persimmons into 1/16-inch slices on a mandoline. Discard the first bottom slices, which are mostly skin. Also discard any seeds.

3. Put the fennel, persimmons, and scallions in a medium bowl. Toss with the olive oil then with the lime juice.

4. Season with fleur de sel and pepper and serve.

GRUYÈRE SALAD WITH WALNUTS AND FRISÉE

4 TO 6 FIRST-COURSE SERVINGS, OR 2 TO 4 LUNCH SALADS

½ cup (2 ounces by weight) walnut pieces

6 ounces Gruyère cheese, rind removed, cut into 3-inch-long sticks, each about ⅛-inch thick

small head of frisée salad, washed and spun dry

1 recipe Mustard Vinaigrette (see p. 78)

2 scallions, green tops removed, thinly sliced

A recipe for Gruyère salad in an Alsatian cookbook inspired this one. My husband and I once served the French version as a snack during a sausage-making party, a slight overkill considering the sausage tasting that was to come. The original is hearty indeed—it contains only *bâtonnets* of cheese, more than three ounces per person, dressed with vinaigrette. Here the addition of walnuts and frisée makes a harmonious and lighter mix, although the cheese is still the main player.

A mustard vinaigrette made with a medium or robust extra-virgin olive oil (see recipe, p. 78) brings out the nuttiness of the cheese.

1. To toast the walnuts, preheat the oven to 350°F. Arrange the walnuts in a single layer in a small pan and roast until you can just detect their aroma and they are lightly browned, about 5 minutes. Let them cool to room temperature. (This can be done ahead.)

2. Put the cheese in a large bowl. Tear the frisée into bite-size pieces. Add enough frisée to approximate twice the volume of the cheese.

3. Toss the cheese and frisée with the vinaigrette. Add the walnuts and scallions (adding them last keeps them from falling to the bottom) and toss a few more times.

4. Serve with crusty bread.

SAUTÉED FRISÉE WITH OLIVE OIL FRIED EGGS

4 FIRST-COURSE SERVINGS, OR 2 LIGHT LUNCH SERVINGS

1 large or 2 medium heads frisée (about 1 pound)

2 tablespoons (1 ounce) robust extra-virgin olive oil

1 small shallot, peeled and finely chopped

1/8 teaspoon dried red chile flakes

fine sea salt and freshly ground black pepper

2 tablespoons (1 ounce) delicate extra-virgin olive oil

4 fresh large eggs

fleur de sel

This is a new take on a rustic French preparation and makes a nice first course or a light lunch accompanied by crusty bread. Traditionally, dandelion greens are wilted with diced smoked bacon and its cooking fat and served as a salad. Depending on the greens, the dish can be refreshingly bracing or extraordinarily bitter. For a more consistent result, I've used the less-bitter frisée. Cooking softens the texture and taste. The greens are cooked in extra-virgin olive oil instead of bacon fat, then topped with fried eggs also cooked in extra-virgin olive oil.

1. Wash the frisée and shake it dry. If the leaves are large, tear them in half.

2. Heat the robust extra-virgin olive oil in a large skillet over medium-high heat until it trembles, becomes aromatic, and a drop of water sputters when it hits the oil. Add the frisée, shallot, and red chile flakes. Sprinkle with salt and a few grindings of pepper. Cover the pan and reduce the heat to medium. Cook until the frisée is wilted and tender, about 5 minutes.

3. Keep the frisée warm while you fry the eggs.

4. In a skillet large enough to hold all the eggs, heat the delicate extra-virgin olive oil over medium heat until it trembles, becomes aromatic, and easily coats the bottom of the skillet. Crack the eggs into the skillet and fry until the whites are opaque and the yolks are just set. If you like firm yolks, cook a little longer.

5. Distribute the frisée on four serving plates. Top each with an egg. Sprinkle with fleur de sel and a few grindings of fresh pepper. Serve immediately.

QUINOA SALAD WITH PISTACHIOS AND CRANBERRIES

4 SERVINGS

⅓ cup (1½ ounces by weight) pistachio nuts

1 cup (6¼ ounces by weight) quinoa

1½ cups (12 ounces) water

½ teaspoon fine sea salt

2 stalks celery, sliced

3 scallions, green tops removed, sliced

¼ cup (1¼ ounces by weight) dried cranberries, coarsely chopped

1 recipe Sherry Vinaigrette (see p. 79)

The colors in this salad will add a festive note to a holiday meal—and it can be prepared in advance so the cooks can devote last-minute preparations to the main course.

Quinoa, native to the Andes Mountains, is related to the weed lambs quarters and has been part of the diet of the people who live on the mountain plateaus of Peru, Bolivia, Ecuador, and Chile for five thousand years. It is a highly nutritious food with protein that is superior to other more common cereal grains. Best of all, it has a nutty, earthy taste.

A vinaigrette made with a medium extra-virgin olive oil and sherry vinegar complements the nutty quinoa and pistachios.

1. To toast the pistachio nuts, preheat the oven to 350°F. Arrange the pistachio nuts in a single layer in a small pan and roast until you can just detect their aroma and they are lightly browned, about 5 minutes. Let them cool to room temperature, then chop them coarsely. (This can be done ahead.)

2. Toast the quinoa in a medium skillet over high heat, shaking the pan occasionally, until it lightly browns, starts to crackle, and smells a bit toasted, about 5 minutes. Transfer to a pot, add the water and the salt, cover, and bring to a simmer. Cook until the quinoa is soft but still has a little bite, about 15 minutes. The water should be gone.

3. Transfer the grain to a bowl and let it cool. Add the pistachio nuts, celery, scallions, and cranberries and toss everything together.

4. Dress with Sherry Vinaigrette.

5. If not serving immediately, refrigerate the salad, but bring it to room temperature before serving.

PRESERVED MEYER LEMONS

1 PINT

About 2 pounds Meyer lemons

¼ cup (2 ounces) fine sea salt

1 bay leaf

This recipe is also great with Eureka lemons, the variety most commonly stocked in stores.

1. Cut 3 lemons (or enough to make about 9 ounces) into quarters. Remove any visible seeds. Put them in a bowl and toss with the salt.

2. Put the bay leaf in the bottom of a clean pint jar. Tightly pack the lemon quarters in the jar. Add any salt remaining in the bowl.

3. Juice about a pound of the remaining lemons. Pour the juice over the lemons in the jar, making sure that all are covered. Juice more of the remaining lemons if needed. Press a round of parchment paper on top of the lemons to keep them submerged. Affix a lid and refrigerate for 1 month before using. The lemons will keep for several months in the refrigerator.

TABBOULEH WITH MEYER LEMON OLIVE OIL

4 TO 6 SERVINGS

½ cup (2⅓ ounces by weight) fine bulgur

1 cup finely chopped flat-leaf parsley leaves (1 large bunch)

½ cup chopped fresh mint leaves

½ cup thinly sliced scallions

1 pint cherry tomatoes, halved

2 tablespoons rinsed, finely chopped preserved Meyer lemons (see p. 102)

⅓ cup (2⅔ ounces) Meyer lemon juice

½ cup (4 ounces) Meyer lemon olive oil

fine sea salt and freshly ground black pepper

leaves of a sturdy lettuce such as Romaine

Meyer lemon oil and Meyer lemon juice give a special sparkle to this traditional salad. Adding preserved Meyer lemons (see previous recipe) intensifies the citrus taste.

This dish is really about the greens. Don't skimp on the parsley or mint. The bulgur gives the salad some heft and offers a crunchy contrast.

Bulgur—wheat berries that have been cooked, dried, and milled—is available in Middle Eastern stores, health-food stores, and some supermarkets.

Tabbouleh can be served immediately, but letting it sit for a few hours melds the flavors and lets the bulgur absorb the lemon juice and olive oil.

1. Put the bulgur in a bowl and add enough cold water to cover it by about 1 inch. Soak for 15 minutes. Line a sieve with cheese-cloth. Pour the soaked bulgur into the lined sieve. Gather the bulgur in the cheesecloth and squeeze it dry.

2. Put the bulgur in a bowl. Add the parsley, mint, scallions, tomatoes, and chopped lemons and toss together. Add the lemon juice and mix with a spatula. Add the Meyer lemon olive oil and mix again. Season with salt and pepper.

3. Line a salad bowl with lettuce leaves, mound the tabbouleh on top, and serve.

APPLE AND PARSNIP SOUP

4 TO 6 SERVINGS

3 tablespoons (1½ ounces) delicate extra-virgin olive oil

2 leeks, washed, with green tops removed, thinly sliced

1 pound parsnips (2 or 3 medium) peeled and cut into 1-inch dice

fine sea salt and freshly ground black pepper

2 large garlic cloves, peeled and finely sliced

1 teaspoon fresh thyme leaves

5 cups homemade or good-quality chicken stock

1½ pounds (about 4) apples, peeled, cored, and cut into 1-inch dice

3 tablespoons (1½ ounces) robust extra-virgin olive oil for drizzling

1½ tablespoons snipped chives

Look for crisp apples with a hint of sweetness for this soup. Locally grown varieties found at farmers' markets will be more flavorful than supermarket fruits that are grown for their shipping and keeping qualities. This is a good first course for a fall meal.

An immersion blender makes short work of turning this soup into a purée.

Use a delicate extra-virgin olive oil, perhaps one with floral or tropical notes such as Ascolano, to cook the soup, then drizzle robust extra-virgin olive oil on the surface before serving, which will contrast perfectly with the soup's sweetness.

1. Heat the delicate olive oil in a medium casserole over medium heat until it trembles, becomes aromatic, and easily coats the bottom of the casserole. Add the leeks and parsnips. Season with salt and pepper. Cook until the leeks are wilted, but not browned, about 5 minutes. Add the garlic and thyme and cook for 2 more minutes.

2. Add the chicken stock and the apples. Bring to a simmer, cover, and cook until the parsnips and apples are falling apart, 35 to 40 minutes.

3. Purée the soup with an immersion blender. Adjust seasoning if necessary.

4. Ladle the soup into hot bowls. Drizzle with robust oil and garnish with snipped chives.

ESCAROLE SOUP WITH BACON

4 SERVINGS

3 tablespoons (1½ ounces) robust extra-virgin olive oil

1 medium-sized onion (about 8 ounces), peeled and finely chopped

2 celery stalks, thinly sliced

2 garlic cloves, peeled and finely sliced

fine sea salt and freshly ground black pepper

⅛ teaspoon dried red chile flakes, or more to taste

5 cups homemade or good-quality chicken stock

2 (about 12 ounces) starchy potatoes, peeled and cut into 1-inch cubes

1 large head (about 12 ounces) escarole, washed, shaken dry, and roughly chopped

4 slices bacon, preferably apple-wood smoked

3 tablespoons (1½ ounces) robust extra-virgin olive oil for drizzling

A cold winter day—especially a snowy one—is a good time to make this soup. Serve it with crusty country bread for a warming lunch. The chile flakes can stand up to a robust extra-virgin olive oil.

1. Heat the olive oil in a large casserole over medium heat until it trembles, becomes aromatic, and easily coats the bottom of the casserole. Add the onion, celery, and garlic. Season with salt and pepper. Cover the casserole, turn the heat to low, and cook until the onions release their moisture and become translucent, about 10 minutes.

2. Sprinkle with the red chile flakes. Add stock, potatoes, and escarole. Season again with salt and pepper if needed. Bring to a simmer, cover, and cook until the potatoes fall apart and the escarole is tender, about 40 minutes.

3. While the soup is cooking, fry the bacon until crisp. Drain on a paper towel. When it is cool, break the slices into small pieces.

4. Ladle the soup into hot bowls. Drizzle with robust oil and garnish with the bacon bits.

OLIVAS DE ORO

4625 La Panza Road
Creston, California 93432
866 556 5483
www.ororganics.com

Frank Menacho hadn't been to many of the California Olive Oil taste panel sessions in the last year, and when I ran into him at the 2007 Paso Robles Olive Oil Festival, I understood why. He and his wife had sold the 160-acre olive oil ranch near Oroville, California, that they purchased in 1999 and bought property just outside Paso Robles, a move they had wanted to make for a couple of years. The new land was bare, but Frank took that in stride. Instead of starting over with all young trees, he decided to move some of the existing trees from Oroville, a distance of 366 miles. The trees, mostly Mission with some Sevillano, were ninety-six years old. He had relocated mature trees for other people, so he was familiar with the intricacies of such a venture, but this was a massive undertaking—he moved two thousand of them.

First the trees needed a heavy pruning so they could clear the freeway overpasses en route: a total of 650 cords of firewood re-sulted. Next they had to be uprooted. Frank and his crew dug deep trenches on all sides of the trees, then hoisted them onto flatbed trucks, wrapped the roots, and secured them. These venerable specimens were loaded onto double trailers, eight per load, and driven south.

I visited the new ranch on a scorching August day. Frank had just climbed down from his tractor, removing the respirator he wears to keep his allergies at bay and taking off his long-sleeved sun-protective shirt. "I'm looking into a cab with air-conditioning," he said. We got into his heavy-duty ranch truck and jounced along, trailing dust behind. The ground was barren, save for the transplanted trees, and a steady wind blew—images of a moonscape came to mind. The irrigation system had yet to be installed, so Frank drove a water tanker from tree to tree. The trees were adapting to their new home; most had new growth, and several had olives.

In addition to mature trees, Frank planted fifteen acres of super-high-density-spaced Arbequina trees. Although the moved trees are certified organic, the new plantings, which were not organically raised, will have to wait three years for certification. He showed me plans for a state-of-the-art pressing facility, a visitor center, and a home site for his family overlooking the orchard.

Frank's previous occupation was good training for this new venture. He owned Westside Fish Market, a commercial fishing and wholesale fish business. While making deliveries to restaurants, he often talked with the chefs about recipes. Many involved olive oil, and they tasted back and forth, choosing oils that went best with the fish. Frank started blending oils to get the taste he wanted. He was smitten with the possibilities.

During the last milling season, still in Oroville, Olivas de Oro entered oils in the Los Angeles competition. Their Meyer lemon oil, made from crushing the citrus from their own organic trees with the olives, won a gold medal. Three other oils, a Mission blend, a Sevillano, and a basil oil made from estate-grown organic basil that was flash-frozen and milled with the olives, all garnered silver medals. And the rosemary olive oil took a bronze.

He moved some of the Meyer lemon trees too. If he doesn't have enough fruit for this season's lemon oil, he has a source of organic citrus.

CORTO OLIVE

11292 North Alpine Road
Stockton, California 95212
209 948 0792
www.corto-olive.com

The first thing I noticed when I entered the office of Corto Olive was a bookcase in the corner. Its four shelves didn't hold books, though; they were filled with bottles of supermarket-brand olive oils, most imported. Surely Corto wasn't using these as models, I thought. When I asked about them, Brady Whitlow, the company's president, explained that they buy them and test them in their lab down the hall. Many had taste defects or acidity levels too high to qualify as true extra-virgin olive oil, despite the claims on the labels. Even more egregious, some oils packaged for the restaurant industry were adulterated—they weren't 100 percent olive oil. Gino Cortopassi, a principal owner of the company, is outraged at these deceptions and hopes that the California olive oil industry will pressure the government to fix the labeling problem.

In 2006, Corto made a test run of their new equipment, from riding harvesters to see how it was done to starting the presses: two hammer mills, a Pieralisi and a Westfalia, each capable of processing eight tons of olives an hour; two malaxation tanks, one with four chambers, the other with three; and horizontal decanters and vertical centrifuges that can handle the constant flow as the olive paste makes its way into oil. To date, this is the largest mill in California. The first run produced a mere 3,000 gallons of oil. In 2008, the projection is 40,000 gallons; the next year, 120,000 gallons. Their target volume is 600,000 gallons.

Even though the noisiest part of the operation is outside the building, the roar of machinery inside precludes conversation at a normal volume. I climbed a steel ladder to peer inside one of the malaxation chambers, where slowly rotating paddles coaxed oil out of the green-brown paste. The finished oil poured from a spigot off the vertical centrifuge like water from a fire hydrant. It was the color of pea soup and had a vegetal olive taste with a slight pungency.

For every ton of olives processed, there are about eighteen hundred pounds of by-products (vegetable water, pomace, and pits), and they can't just be dumped on the ground. At Corto, an auger pushes this mass outside the building, where it goes into containers to be sold for cattle feed. But first it gets one last treatment: the pits are removed. "It makes it easier for the cows to eat." Brady told me. They thought of composting it, but it takes time to decompose, and they don't have the acreage to accommodate it all.

Although both Corto and the California Olive Ranch (see p. 130) are focused on super-high density plantings to produce extra-virgin olive oil at an affordable price, their business models differ. Corto strives to become the most reliable source of private-label extra-virgin olive oil in California. It plans to sell bulk oil to repackers, who will do their own branding, marketing, and sales. Brady thinks this is more profitable than selling the oil under their own label. "Competi-

tion for supermarket shelf space is tough," he said. Eventually he plans to bottle and label oil for private customers. (The bottling line was still a construction site the day I visited.) Corto would process oil and sell it for the growers, minus production fees, unlike California Olive Ranch, who contracts with growers at a set price. But like California Olive Ranch, Corto is looking for growers, encouraging people with low-profit vineyards to pull out the vines and plant olives.

Brady thinks there is room for both systems. The less expensive, and usually lesser-quality, imported oil is the competition.

FISH

Extra-virgin olive oil plays many roles in these recipes—it acts as a cooking medium, it preserves, it garnishes, and it helps emulsify a sauce. Perhaps olive oil goes so well with fish because they are both major components of the Mediterranean diet.

I have included two recipes for salt cod, a fish widely used throughout the region. If you have never cooked with it, I encourage you to try these recipes. It may seem odd to use salted fish that needs to be reconstituted in water before cooking when quick transport and refrigeration provide an ample supply of fresh fish, but its taste is distinct and complex. The difference between the two is comparable to that between fresh and cured meat.

SALMON WITH BASIL OLIVE OIL BAKED IN PARCHMENT

4 SERVINGS

1½ pounds Coho salmon filet, about 1 inch thick

fine sea salt and freshly ground pepper

1 medium (about 6 ounces) sweet onion, such as Walla Walla, cut into halves and thinly sliced

4 ounces (15 to 20) cherry tomatoes, halved

2 tablespoons (1 ounce) basil olive oil

Fish aficionados on the west coast eagerly await the start of the prized King salmon (also called Chinook) season each year, which coincides with the slowdown of the Dungeness crab catch, another local favorite. In the spring of 2008 they were disappointed, but not nearly as devastated as the fishermen, because the season was closed due to the drastically low numbers of fish returning to the rivers to spawn. I made the best of this misfortune by trying other types of salmon, including the leaner Coho. The method of cooking—enclosed in a parchment package with a drizzle of olive oil—keeps this leaner fish moist. King salmon, although richer, would also be tasty prepared the same way.

1. Preheat the oven to 400°F.

2. Put a piece of parchment paper about twice the size of the fish on a baking pan. (If the fish is too large to fit into one paper package, or if you have more than one piece, make two packages.)

3. Salt and pepper the fish on both sides. Put the fish, skin side down, on the parchment paper. Strew the onion slices and tomatoes over the fish. Drizzle with olive oil. Fold the edges of the parchment so the ends meet, and pleat them at 1-inch intervals to seal in the fish.

4. Bake until the parchment starts to turn brown, about 15 minutes. To test the fish for doneness, insert an instant-read thermometer through the parchment into the thickest part of the fish. It should read between 125 and 130°F. If the fish isn't cooked, return it to the oven for a few more minutes and test again.

5. Transfer the pouch to a serving dish and take it to the table. Open the parchment and serve each guest a portion of fish without the skin and with a few spoonfuls of cooking liquid.

TUNA POACHED IN EXTRA-VIRGIN OLIVE OIL

4 TO 6 SERVINGS

1 pound albacore tuna

fine sea salt and freshly ground black pepper

1/2 teaspoon dried herbes de Provence, lightly crushed with the fingers

about 1 cup (8 ounces) medium extra-virgin olive oil

Judy Rodgers of Zuni Cafe in San Francisco has what she terms a "Sunday night fish problem" (the restaurant is closed on Mondays). She solves it by cooking any unsold ahi tuna in olive oil to extend its shelf life. Then she uses it in various appetizer dishes or tosses it with pasta.

Delfina Pizzeria, also in San Francisco, gives albacore tuna the same treatment and mixes it with beans as a starter.

Use the tuna the way the restaurants do, or in a Niçoise salad, Pan Bagnat (see recipe, p. 53), Tonnato sauce (see recipe, p. 190), or in any dish that calls for canned tuna. (This will be far superior.)

1. Cut the tuna into 1/2-inch slices. Rub all over with salt, pepper, and the herbs. Tightly arrange the fish in a pot that will just accommodate the pieces. Add olive oil until the fish is submerged.

2. Bring to a gentle simmer so that there is a steady stream of small bubbles around the perimeter of the pan. Don't bring to a rolling boil.

3. Cover the pan and cook until the fish registers 170°F on an instant-read thermometer, about 45 minutes.

4. Transfer the fish to a plate and cool to room temperature. Pour the oil into another container and let it cool to room temperature as well.

5. When cool, pack the fish into a container just large enough to hold it. Add the oil. If the fish isn't covered, add a little more extra-virgin olive oil.

6. Cover and refrigerate. The fish will keep for 5 days. When you have used all the fish, discard the oil.

SALT COD BAKED WITH LEEKS AND POTATOES

4 TO 6 SERVINGS

1 pound good-quality salt cod

1 bay leaf

4 tablespoons (2 ounces) delicate extra-virgin olive oil, divided, plus more for the baking dish

2 garlic cloves, thinly sliced

2 tablespoons unbleached all-purpose flour

2 cups (16 ounces) hot water

1 tablespoon chopped fresh tarragon

1/2 teaspoon fine sea salt

freshly ground black pepper

3 leeks, washed, green tops removed, sliced into 1/4-inch rounds

3 medium-sized waxy potatoes (about 12 ounces), peeled and sliced, preferably on a mandoline, into 1/16-inch rounds

While vacationing in Barcelona a few years ago, I saw an astounding array of salt cod for sale at the market, La Boqueria, just off La Rambla, a bustling street. Cuts from different parts of the fish were displayed; the choicest pieces were the thicker ones, and they were priced accordingly. The fish was available salted or presoaked so it could be cooked immediately. Not having a kitchen at my disposal, I could only admire and dream about cooking possibilities. Back home in San Francisco, I bought salt cod and headed to the kitchen.

Buy good-quality salt cod, not the dried out hard-as-a-brick pieces sometimes seen in ethnic markets. The cod sold in wooden boxes is acceptable. The taste of salt cod is distinctive—a little more pronounced than fresh fish, but not strong. I like to pair it with a delicate oil because that doesn't interfere with the fish's unique taste.

The fish needs to desalt in cold water, so start two days before you plan to serve the dish.

1. Soak the salt cod in cold water in the refrigerator, changing the water four times, for 48 hours.

2. After soaking, drain the fish, put it in a saucepan, cover with water, and bring to a boil. Skim any foam from the surface. Add the bay leaf. Turn the heat to low and maintain a slow simmer until the fish is tender and flakes with a fork, 50 to 60 minutes, skimming foam as necessary. The cooking time will vary with the dryness and quality of the fish. Taste a piece to be sure that it is tender.

3. Remove the fish from the pan. Let it cool, then carefully separate it into flakes, removing any skin, membranes, or bones (hands do this job best). This can be done up to 1 day ahead. Cover and store in the refrigerator.

4. Preheat the oven to 425°F.

5. Heat 2 tablespoons of the extra-virgin olive oil in a medium saucepan over high heat until it trembles, becomes aromatic, and easily coats the bottom of the pan. Add the garlic, turn the heat to low, and cook until the garlic softens, but does not brown, a minute or two. Whisk the flour into the pan and cook until it bubbles, about 1 minute. Add the hot water and tarragon. Bring to a boil and whisk over medium-low heat until the sauce thickens, 3 to 5 minutes. Whisk in the salt and a few grindings of black pepper.

6. Lightly oil a medium-size gratin dish or *cazuela*. Layer the leeks in one layer on the bottom, then cover them with the fish in one layer. Overlap the potato slices on top, making two layers of them.

7. Pour the hot sauce over the fish and vegetables. Drizzle the remaining 2 tablespoons of extra-virgin olive oil on top.

8. Bake until the potatoes are tender and the top is browned and bubbling, 45 to 50 minutes.

9. Serve on warm plates.

ESCABECHE

8 FIRST-COURSE OR 4 MAIN-COURSE SERVINGS

2/3 cup (5 1/4 ounces) medium extra-virgin olive oil, divided

fine sea salt

1 1/2 pounds fresh cod or halibut filets, about 1/2- to 3/4-inch thick

2 medium onions (about 1 pound), peeled, cut into halves, and thinly sliced

1 large carrot (5 ounces), peeled and cut into thin slices

freshly ground black pepper

3 garlic cloves, peeled and thinly sliced

1 bay leaf

1/2 small chipotle pepper, seeds and ribs removed

1/3 cup (2 2/3 ounces) white wine vinegar

This basic idea, frying fish and then marinating it in olive oil and vinegar, is used in many parts of the world where fish is plentiful—the Mediterranean, the coast of Portugal, and in Latin America. It's a dish that is best made ahead so the flavors can mingle (although I have consumed it with pleasure two hours after it was prepared). It would be perfect for a picnic.

Because this is essentially a pickled dish, the vinegar needs a medium extra-virgin olive oil for balance.

Don't be tempted to use sablefish—it is sometimes called black cod, but it is not cod and it has a softer texture.

1. Heat 1/3 cup of the extra-virgin olive oil in a medium skillet over high heat until it trembles, becomes aromatic, and a drop of water sputters when it hits the oil. Turn the heat to medium, sprinkle the fish with salt, and sauté it without crowding until it is opaque and flaking, 3 to 5 minutes a side, depending on the thickness of the fish. Cook in batches if necessary. Transfer the cooked fish to a plate and reserve.

2. Either wash the skillet or use another one. Heat the remaining 1/3 cup extra-virgin olive oil over medium heat until it trembles and becomes aromatic. Add the onions and carrot. Sprinkle with salt and a few grindings of pepper. Cook, stirring frequently, until the onions are translucent and just starting to color, about 10 minutes.

3. Add the garlic, bay leaf, chipotle pepper, and vinegar. Bring to a simmer and cook until the onions are very soft and the carrots tender, about 10 more minutes. Taste for salt and pepper.

4. Pour any liquid that has accumulated under the reserved fish into the pan and bring to a boil.

5. Arrange the fish in one layer in a serving dish deep enough to accommodate the sauce. Pour the hot sauce over the fish.

6. Cool to room temperature, then refrigerate for up to 4 days, until ready to serve. Bring to room temperature before serving.

SAUTÉED SHRIMP WITH A SHELL-BASED SAUCE

4 SERVINGS

6 tablespoons (3 ounces) delicate extra-virgin olive oil, divided, plus more for drizzling over the finished dish

1½ pounds fresh shrimp, peeled and deveined, shells reserved

1 tablespoon Pernod, or another pastis

2 cups (16 ounces) water

fine sea salt and freshly ground black pepper

This easy preparation lets the sweetness of the shrimp shine. Use wild-caught shrimp in their shells from Louisiana or Florida for the best taste. The flavorful shells are the base for a simple sauce. A delicate olive oil with some buttery flavor best complements the shrimp.

Serve the cooked shrimp over a bed of steamed rice and sautéed onions and peppers.

1. Heat 3 tablespoons of the extra-virgin olive oil in a large skillet over high heat until it trembles, becomes aromatic, and a drop of water sputters when it hits the oil. Add the shrimp shells and toss them in the oil until they turn red, a few minutes. Reduce the heat to medium. Add the Pernod, ignite the alcohol by tilting the pan over a gas flame or using a match, and shake the pan until the flames die. Add the water and bring to a simmer. Turn the heat to low and cover the pan. Simmer for 15 minutes. Strain through a sieve into a bowl, pressing down on the shells. Reserve the liquid.

2. Heat 3 more tablespoons of the extra-virgin olive oil over high heat in a skillet large enough to hold the shrimp in one layer. When the oil trembles, becomes aromatic, and a drop of water sputters when it hits the oil, add the shrimp and salt them. Cook until the sides in the oil turn pink. Turn the shrimp over, add the reserved liquid, and bring to a boil. Adjust the salt. Cook until the shrimp turn red, about a minute. Don't overcook them.

3. Spoon the fish and sauce over rice and vegetables. Season with freshly ground pepper and a drizzle of extra-virgin olive oil. Serve immediately.

ANCHOVY CRUDO WITH LEMON OLIVE OIL

4 TO 6 SERVINGS

1 pound very fresh anchovies

1 Meyer or Eureka lemon, halved

$1/4$ cup (2 ounces) Meyer lemon or Eureka lemon olive oil

fleur de sel and freshly ground black pepper

Fresh anchovies with a squeeze of lemon and a few drops of lemon olive oil bear no resemblance to those packed in jars or tins. Even people who are wary of raw fish might take to these.

Good fish markets often have anchovies or will order them. Call ahead to make sure they will be available when you want them. It takes a little practice to clean the fish, although it might seem clumsy at first, it doesn't take long to get into a rhythm.

Serve the anchovy filets on toasted baguette slices with an aperitif as a first course with a small salad, or on a pissaladière. Or add them to a fish stew.

1. Lay newspapers out on a work surface. Check the fish for scales. If there are any, remove them by gently scraping the fish from tail to head with the flat side of a paring knife blade. Be careful not to cut the skin.

2. Grasp a fish, belly facing you, just behind the head. Hold the body of the fish in the palm of your other hand and insert the thumb of that hand through the belly to the spine just behind the head. Use your index finger to steady the fish as you run your thumb from head to tail, opening up the fish.

3. Lay the fish, skin side down, on the newspaper. Break the spine where it joins the head and gently coax it from the meat. Twist off the head; the entrails should come away with it. You will now have two filets with skin intact.

4. Rinse the filets and lay them on paper towels or a kitchen towel to drain while you clean the rest of the fish. Gently pat them dry.

5. Put half of the filets on a plate in a single layer. Squeeze the juice from a lemon half over the fish. Repeat with the rest on another plate.

6. Cover with plastic wrap and refrigerate until ready to serve, or up to 4 hours.

7. Before serving, drizzle with lemon olive oil and sprinkle with fleur de sel and a few grindings of pepper.

VARIATION:
SALTED ANCHOVIES

You can serve half the filets moistened with lemon juice and lemon olive oil and preserve half for later by salting them.

1. Put a single layer of filets (without lemon juice) in a shallow bowl and cover with fine sea salt. Continue layering and salting until all the fish are covered with salt. You will need about ½ cup salt.

2. Cover the bowl and refrigerate for 24 hours. Drain the accumulated liquid from the bowl, re-cover it, and return it to the refrigerator until ready to use, or up to 2 weeks.

3. Before serving, rinse the salt from the filets, pat them dry, drizzle with medium extra-virgin olive oil, and add a few grindings of pepper.

CALAMARI STEW WITH RED WINE

8 FIRST-COURSE OR 4 MAIN-COURSE SERVINGS

- 2 pounds cleaned small squid, a mix of tubes and tentacles
- fine sea salt and freshly ground black pepper
- 5 tablespoons (2¹/₂ ounces) medium or robust extra-virgin olive oil, divided
- 3 celery stalks, thinly sliced
- 2 leeks, washed, green tops removed, cut in half lengthwise and thinly sliced
- 3 garlic cloves, peeled and thinly sliced
- 1³/₄ cups (14 ounces) dry red wine
- ¹/₄ teaspoon dried red chile flakes
- 1 tablespoon tomato paste
- 1 bay leaf
- slices of crusty bread

Calamari can be tricky. They will be tender if cooked for a minute or for forty-five minutes. Any cooking time in between will leave them tough. This recipe uses the slow-cooked method.

This stew is dark and rich from the red wine. Although made with fish, it is a hearty dish. Serve it on a toasted slice of crusty bread.

1. Cut the squid tubes into ¹/₂-inch rounds. Pat the rounds and tentacles with a kitchen towel to dry them.

2. Heat 3 tablespoons of the extra-virgin olive oil over high heat in a medium casserole until it trembles, becomes aromatic, and a drop of water sputters when it hits the oil. Add one third of the squid rounds and salt them. Cook, stirring, until they become firm and opaque, about a minute. Remove the squid to a dish. Cook the remaining squid rounds in two batches, then cook the tentacles.

3. Add the remaining 2 tablespoons extra-virgin olive oil to the pan. Heat over medium heat until the oil trembles, becomes aromatic, and easily coats the bottom of the pan. Add the celery, leeks, and garlic. Sprinkle with salt and pepper. Cover the casserole, reduce the heat to low, and cook until the vegetables are wilted, but not brown, about 5 minutes.

4. Add the wine and bring to a simmer.

5. Add the chile flakes, tomato paste, and bay leaf.

6. Return the squid and any accumulated juices to the casserole. Bring to a simmer, cover, and cook over low heat until the squid is very tender, 45 to 50 minutes. Taste for seasoning, then serve in warm bowls atop toasted slices of crusty bread.

BACALAO AL PIL PIL

4 SERVINGS

1½ pounds salt cod, with skin attached, preferably the tenderloin (see La Tienda in Resources)

½ cup (4 ounces) medium extra-virgin olive oil

2 large garlic cloves, peeled and sliced

I once saw a cook in a tapas bar in San Sebastián intently swirling a pan that contained a piece of fish and olive oil over low heat. He was making *pil pil*, the Basque word for "bubbling" that is onomatopoeic in describing the sound the oil makes as this classic dish cooks. The dish wasn't on the menu, and when it was finished the cook took the pan and disappeared into a back room. I had to wait until I returned home to make it. The emulsion sauce that forms from the olive oil and the albumin in the fish skin is magical, and so is the taste. It takes time for the emulsion to develop. Don't despair; keep swirling.

The fish needs to desalt in cold water, so start two days before you plan to serve the dish.

1. Soak the salt cod in cold water in the refrigerator, changing the water four times, for 48 hours. Remove the fish from the water, cut it into four serving pieces, and pat it dry.

2. Heat the extra-virgin olive oil in a large skillet over medium heat until it trembles, becomes aromatic, and easily coats the bottom of the skillet. Add the garlic and cook until the garlic is lightly browned, about 1 minute. Remove and discard the garlic and set about half of the oil aside. Let the oil remaining in the skillet cool for 3 to 4 minutes.

3. Turn the heat to medium. Add the fish, skin side up. Adjust the heat so that the olive oil just simmers, swirling the pan every 2 to 3 minutes. When the fish is almost cooked through (it becomes opaque), 7 to 10 minutes, turn it skin side down. (The cooking time will depend on the thickness of the fish.) Continue swirling the pan every 2 to 3 minutes. When the fish is completely opaque, turn up the heat to medium. Add the reserved olive oil (not the garlic) back to the pan a tablespoon at a time, swirling continuously. Continue until a white sauce forms, a few more minutes.

4. Serve on hot plates, advising diners to watch for bones.

FISH STEW WITH AÏOLI

4 SERVINGS

¼ teaspoon saffron threads

2¼ cups (18 ounces) water, divided

4 tablespoons (2 ounces) delicate or medium extra-virgin olive oil, divided

12 fresh shrimp (about ½ pound), peeled and deveined, shells reserved

splash of Pernod or another pastis

1 leek, washed, green top removed, cut into ¼-inch rounds

1 garlic clove, peeled and finely chopped

½ green poblano pepper, ribs and seeds removed, cut into ½-inch strips

fine sea salt

¾ pound small waxy potatoes, peeled and quartered

1 pound rock cod filets, cut into 1-inch strips

1 pound mussels, beards removed

freshly ground black pepper

1 recipe Aïoli (see recipe, p. 84)

A dollop of aïoli adds another dimension to this flavorful fish stew. Use wild-caught shrimp from Louisiana or Florida for the best taste. Buy mussels with dark, glistening shells. Sometimes mussels gape a little; if the shells close when pinched together, they are still alive. Discard any open shells that do not do this.

Pernod and saffron speak of the south of France, and the poblano pepper, although not regional, contributes a spicy undertone.

1. Heat a small skillet over high heat. When a drop of water dances on the surface, add the saffron and shake the pan until the threads become brittle, about 30 seconds. Transfer them to a mortar and grind them to a powder with a pestle. Heat ¼ cup of the water, pour it over the saffron threads, and set aside.

2. Heat 2 tablespoons of the extra-virgin olive oil in a large skillet over high heat until it trembles, becomes aromatic, and a drop of water sputters when it hits the oil. Add the shrimp shells and toss them in the oil until they turn red, a few minutes. Reduce the heat to medium. Add the Pernod, ignite the alcohol by tilting the pan over a gas flame or using a match, and shake the pan until the flames die. Add the remaining 2 cups water, turn the heat to low, and cover the pan. Simmer for 15 minutes. Strain through a sieve into a bowl, pressing down on the shells. Reserve the liquid.

3. Heat the remaining 2 tablespoons extra-virgin olive oil in a large saucepan or a large, 2-inch deep skillet over medium heat until it trembles and becomes aromatic. Add the leek, garlic, and pepper strips and sprinkle with salt. Reduce the heat to low, cover, and cook until the vegetables begin to soften, about 5 minutes.

4. Pour the saffron-infused liquid and the reserved shrimp-shell liquid into the saucepan. Bring to a boil. Add the potatoes and sprinkle them with salt. Lower the heat to medium, cover the pan, and cook until the potatoes are almost tender, about 20 minutes.

5. Layer the fish filets and shrimp on top of the vegetables, salt again and put the mussels on top. Cover the pan, increase the heat to medium-high, and cook at a brisk simmer until the fish and shrimp are opaque and the mussels are open, 3 to 5 minutes.

6. Ladle into hot bowls, add a few grindings of pepper and a dollop of aïoli to each, and serve immediately.

7. Serve the rest of the aïoli on the side.

OVEN-OPENED OYSTERS WITH LEMON OLIVE OIL

2 TO 4 SERVINGS

2 dozen small or medium fresh oysters in their shells

2 cups (2½ pounds) rock salt

½ cup (4 ounces) Meyer lemon or Eureka lemon olive oil

freshly ground black pepper

I love oysters, but neither my husband nor I are good at prying them open. This recipe lets you forget about your oyster-shucking skills, good or bad—the heat takes the place of an oyster knife.

Olive oil is not a traditional accompaniment for oysters, but a dash of Meyer lemon or Eureka lemon oil tames the bivalves' austereness.

Rock salt in the baking pan steadies the oysters so their juice stays in the shells as they bake.

Serve as a first course. The number of oysters is just a suggestion. Bake more for true aficionados, increasing the rock salt and lemon olive oil accordingly.

1. Preheat oven to 500°F.
2. Pour the rock salt into a baking pan and nestle the oysters in it. (If you are baking more, or if the oysters are medium sized, you may need two pans.)
3. Bake until the oysters just start to open, about 7 minutes.
4. Put sufficient protection on the table, then take the oysters to the table, still in their baking pan.
5. Provide a cruet of lemon olive oil and a peppermill so diners can season them to taste.

CALIFORNIA OLIVE RANCH

2675 Lone Tree Road
Oroville, California 95965
530 846 8000
www.californiaoliveranch.com

Driving down a straight, flat road just south of Oroville, California, I saw the trees. They were not the majestic gnarled trees visible in much of California, Mission and Manzanillo trees planted a hundred years ago. From afar, these almost looked like grape vines—military-precision rows, the branches of one (more shrub than tree) touching the next, all a uniform seven feet tall.

This was the estate orchard of the California Olive Ranch, planted in 1999 according to the super-high-density system developed in Spain about fifteen years ago. Instead of the standard spacing of 120 trees per acre, 670 semidwarf trees were planted cheek by jowl on one acre of land. The advantages are significant. The semi-dwarf trees start producing at least three years earlier than standard trees and, more important, can be harvested mechanically; two people and a machine can strip the olives from an acre of trees in one hour. Hand picking them in the same amount of time would require forty people. The

harvesters are tall, lumbering machines that straddle a row of trees, shaking the olives loose as they pass. The olives travel up a conveyor belt and drop into a tractor-pulled gondola running parallel to the harvester one row over.

To date, there are three varieties of olives that can be dwarfed and planted in this manner: Arbequina and Arbosana, both Spanish in origin, and Koroneiki, a Greek olive. A mixture of the three produces a delicate to medium oil well suited to people starting to use olive oil as well as a favorite of the judges at the Los Angeles competition, where the oils have achieved gold medal recognition.

Alan Greene, the vice president of sales and marketing, has grand plans for the company, but he wasn't always in love with olives. He happily retired after eighteen years at Blue Diamond, a large California almond cooperative. A colleague from Blue Diamond who was consulting with the California Olive Ranch gave him a bottle of the oil. He took it home, but his wife didn't like it. "There's something wrong with this. It doesn't taste like this oil," she said, comparing it to a bottle of supermarket oil. Alan tasted both oils and was stunned by how much better the California Olive Ranch oil was. His wife tried them again and over time became a convert. Now she tries it on food that she wouldn't have considered "BC," that is, before California Olive Ranch. Another recipient of the same oil threw it out.

Alan's consulting friend wanted him to sign on with the company. At first he wouldn't consider it: "I didn't know anything about olives." But in August 2003, as he drove past the almost five hundred acres of the ranch's trees heavily laden with fruit, he was impressed. He toured the mill. Because of his long history in the food business, he had seen his share of production facilities, including old-fashioned, less-than-pristine olive oil operations, and he was impressed by this mill's cleanliness and organization. He realized that he could apply the same business model he had used for almonds. In the 1960s, the California almond industry was a stepchild of Spain; now California produces about 80 percent of the world's almonds. He saw the same potential for olives.

The mill, situated in the middle of the original orchard, is a big operation. Two lines run side by side, one processing three and a half tons of olives an hour, the other seven and a half. The day I was there, we walked to the receiving area just as a truck arrived pulling two brimming hoppers, each holding about eleven tons of olives. The driver positioned the first over a large grate, then he loosened the funnel-shaped bottom of the hopper and green olives rained down. A conveyer moved them to a blower to remove leaves and into a washer. Next they went to the two-phase Pieralisi hammer mills, positioned outside the building because they are so noisy. Inside, malaxation tanks, horizontal centrifuges, and vertical separators would finish the job.

By 2005, the company had signed some growers to augment their crop (an advertisement in the October 2007 issue of the magazine *Olint* offered a nine-dollar-a-gallon guarantee for a twelve-year contract) and had begun looking for acreage to buy. They purchased 800 acres in Artois, about fifty miles to the south. Now they have 1,800 acres planted with 1,220,000 young trees. Eventually, all these olives will need to be processed, so another mill is on the drawing board, one that can add ten-ton-per-hour lines, one at a time as needed.

For the 2008 harvest, California Olive Ranch expects to produce more than 150,000 gallons of oil. (The entire California production will be about 500,000 gallons.) By 2011, they expect production of 500,000 gallons. The prediction for 2113 is twice that—one million gallons of oil. Watch out, Spain. California is catching up!

NURSTECH, INC.

NURSTECH, INC.

612 East Gridley Road
Gridley, California 95948
530 846 0404
www.nurstech.com

NursTech, Inc., just outside the small town of Gridley, California, is fueling the super-high-density olive tree plantings in California. The Spanish parent company, Agromillora, experimented with more than a hundred varieties of trees before coming up with three clones, Arbequina 1-18, Arbosana 1-43, and Koroneiki 1-38, that are suited to this style of planting. The clones were developed through selection and propagation, not genetic modification. It is a time-consuming process. First mother trees are cross-pollinated. Some of the resulting olives are planted. After six or seven years, these seedlings produce fruit. The researchers take cuttings from the most promising trees and plant them in different climates (and countries) in grower trials. Only then are selections made. Selected trees must have a compact shape suitable for mechanical harvesting, the ability to start bearing in two to three years, and the olives must make good oil.

Agromillora, which has a variety of locations, including Spain, Australia, Chile, and Argentina, recruited Xavier Marques to be the executive director of NursTech in 2000. "It was quite a change to move from Barcelona to Gridley," he told me.

The day I visited, he strode from the trailer that serves as an office along with Jeffers Richardson, in charge of marketing, to show me around. There is a long stand of olive trees just inside a chain-link fence that separates the nursery from the road. These are sample trees, each a different variety, sixty-five in all. These trees aren't for sale, but Xavier likes to show them to customers because their shapes and the olives that they produce vary widely. We stopped at each one, and Xavier picked a few olives, pointing out characteristics of the tree. Some squat, some tall and gangly; some loaded with olives, others bare; some with olives in grapelike clusters, others with single fruits spaced along the branches; some with tiny olives (Koroneiki), others with olives the size of plums (Sevillano). There were trees from every olive-producing part of the world, and this was only a small selection.

Some critics think that NursTech is focusing only on Spanish varieties, but Xavier said the company is experimenting with several varieties that can meet the criteria for super-high-density planting. They would like to have a tree that can be harvested as early as September so that it can be planted in climates that are susceptible to fall frosts.

We walked through the enclosed section of the nursery where the cuttings are started. They are pampered here, protected from the wind and heated from the bottom. When they get larger, they are moved outside and, as they grow taller, transplanted to larger pots. The original nursery site was thirty-four acres; they just purchased thirty-nine more to keep up with the demand for these semidwarf trees. When I visited in 2007, there were eight thousand acres of super-high-density trees planted throughout California; at least four thousand more were planned for the next year.

On our way back to the office, we passed workers loading a trailer truck from Sierra Gold nursery with one-foot-tall trees, about a year old, for delivery to a client. Sierra Gold is one of the distributors that sells and delivers the NursTech trees. Spring and fall are the best times to plant, but Xavier told me they sell trees all year long. It's nonstop propagation at NursTech.

VEGETABLES AND SIDE DISHES

This chapter offers a diversity of ideas, from a new way to look at the humble mashed potato to an intriguing Middle Eastern dish with caramelized onions, rice, and lentils. Eggplant is a vegetable that cries out for extra-virgin olive oil; it doesn't taste the same without it. I have experimented with salting eggplant and have decided that this is an unnecessary step, especially if the eggplant is in season and fresh. Salting waterlogs it and lets it soak up too much oil when it is cooked. Frying eggplant, salted or not, also saturates it with oil. Lightly coating it with oil and roasting is a better option.

MASHED POTATOES WITH EXTRA-VIRGIN OLIVE OIL

4 TO 6 SERVINGS

1½ pounds starchy potatoes

1 tablespoon fine sea salt, plus more for serving

about ½ cup (4 ounces) extra-virgin olive oil

freshly ground black pepper

Use a baking potato with high starch content or an all-purpose potato with a medium starch content for this dish, not the waxy varieties that are better in salads. Some possibilities are russets, Kennebecs, or Yukon Golds. Purple-fleshed potatoes are also starchy, but when mashed they take on a drab gray hue. Potatoes are a template for flavor. Traditionally, they are mashed with butter and sometimes buttermilk. Using an extra-virgin olive oil (a delicate one with buttery or even nutty overtones is a good match) instead of a dairy-based addition produces a cleaner, unmasked potato taste.

1. Peel the potatoes. If they are large, cut them in half. Put them in a medium saucepan and cover with cold water. Add 1 tablespoon salt. Bring to a boil and cook until they are tender, 20 to 30 minutes.

2. Drain the potatoes, reserving some of the cooking liquid.

3. Mash the potatoes in the pot over low heat with a masher. Gradually add the olive oil until the potatoes absorb it and become smooth. You may not need it all. If the potatoes absorb all the oil and you want them even smoother, drizzle in about ¼ cup of the reserved cooking liquid.

4. Correct the seasoning and serve.

GARLIC MASHED POTATOES WITH EXTRA-VIRGIN OLIVE OIL

The addition of roasted garlic completely changes the personality of this dish, making it more robust and able to stand up to a more assertive olive oil. Follow the previous recipe with this addition:

1. Preheat the oven to 400°F. Cut the top from a small head of unpeeled garlic, exposing the cloves. While the potatoes are cooking, roast the garlic until the tops of the cloves are soft and lightly browned, about 20 minutes. The cloves will be very soft.

2. Let the garlic cool slightly so you can handle it. Squeeze the cooked garlic out of each clove. Add to the potatoes before mashing.

SPICY EGGPLANT RAGOUT

6 TO 8 SERVINGS

1 eggplant (about 1 pound), peeled and cut into 1-inch cubes

1/2 cup (4 ounces) robust extra-virgin olive oil, divided

fine sea salt and freshly ground black pepper

1 teaspoon dried coriander

1 teaspoon dried cumin

1/2 teaspoon dried red chile flakes

1 large red bell pepper, ribbed, seeded, and cut into 1-inch cubes

1 medium fennel bulb, cut into 1/2-inch slices

2 stalks celery, cut into 1/4-inch slices

1/2 medium onion, peeled and cut into 1/4-inch slices

2 garlic cloves, peeled and finely chopped

3/4 cup (6 ounces) red table wine, plus more if needed

This dish borrows flavors from around the Mediterranean—spices of Africa and fennel from France and pairs them with eggplant, a favorite of the region.

It is best in the late summer and early fall, when eggplant is in season and is not bitter. It is a very versatile dish—accompanying roasted chicken or meat, served over rice, tossed with pasta, or as part of an antipasto.

The spicy character lends itself to a robust oil. If you love spicy food, increase the chile flakes to ¾ teaspoon.

1. Preheat the oven to 400°F and line a baking pan with parchment paper.

2. Put the eggplant cubes in a bowl and toss them with ¼ cup of the extra-virgin olive oil. Sprinkle with salt and a few grindings of pepper.

3. Arrange the cubes in a single layer in the baking pan.

4. Roast the eggplant until lightly browned, about 10 to 15 minutes. Set aside.

5. Heat the remaining ¼ cup of extra-virgin olive oil in a large skillet over high heat until it trembles, becomes aromatic, and easily coats the bottom of the skillet. Add the coriander, cumin, and red chile flakes. Stir until the spices start to brown, 15 to 20 seconds. Add the bell pepper, fennel, celery, onion, and garlic and reduce the heat to medium-low. Sprinkle with salt and cover the pan. Cook until the vegetables are slightly softened but not brown, about 15 minutes.

6. Add the roasted eggplant and the wine. Cover and cook over low heat, adding more wine if the ragout becomes too dry, until all the vegetables are soft, 35 to 40 minutes. Season with salt and pepper as needed.

7. Serve immediately with roasted meat or over rice or pasta, or cool and serve at room temperature as an antipasto.

Individual Vegetable Tians

These vegetable dishes get their name from the traditional shallow earthenware dishes in which they are made. I first discovered tians years ago and now this is a favorite way to cook vegetables. I like to use my *cazuelas*, Spanish earthenware dishes that are glazed on the inside and five inches in diameter. You could also bake them in a larger gratin dish. These make a light first course or side with a meat or fish entree.

TRICOLOR TOMATO TIANS

4 SERVINGS

4 tablespoons (2 ounces) basil olive oil, divided

1 large onion (12 ounces), peeled, cut in half, and sliced

fine sea salt

1 garlic clove, peeled and cut in half

1½ pounds small ripe heirloom tomatoes, red, yellow, and green, such as Early Girl, Taxi, and Green Zebra

fleur de sel and freshly ground black pepper

1. Preheat the oven to 450°F.

2. Heat 2 tablespoons of the basil olive oil in a medium skillet over medium heat until it trembles, becomes aromatic, and easily coats the bottom of the skillet. Add the onion, sprinkle with salt, and cook until it is soft and lightly colored, about 20 minutes. If the onion starts to dry out before it is ready, add a little more oil.

3. Meanwhile, rub the bottoms of the *cazuelas* with the garlic clove. Cut the tomatoes into ¼-inch slices.

4. Distribute the onions evenly in the *cazuelas*. Alternate layers of the tomatoes on top of the onions, making six rows, two of each color. Pack the slices in snugly, overlapping them both horizontally and vertically. They will stand up at a slight angle.

5. Drizzle the remaining basil oil on top of the tomatoes. Sprinkle with fleur de sel and freshly ground black pepper.

6. Bake for 15 minutes. Remove the *cazuelas* and push down on the vegetables with a metal spatula. Return to the oven and bake until the vegetables are soft and starting to caramelize, about 15 more minutes.

7. Serve directly from the *cazuelas*.

YELLOW AND GREEN ZUCCHINI TIANS WITH FRESH THYME

4 SERVINGS

4 tablespoons (2 ounces) medium extra-virgin olive oil, divided

1 large onion (12 ounces), peeled, cut in half, and sliced

fine sea salt

1 garlic clove, peeled and cut in half

4 medium-size zucchinis (about 1¼ pounds), 2 yellow and 2 green, no more than 1½ inches in diameter

1 tablespoon fresh thyme leaves

fleur de sel and freshly ground black pepper

1. Preheat the oven to 450°F.

2. Heat 2 tablespoons of the extra-virgin olive oil in a medium skillet over medium heat until it trembles, becomes aromatic, and easily coats the bottom of the skillet. Add the onion, sprinkle with salt, and cook over medium heat until it is soft and lightly colored, about 20 minutes. If the onion starts to dry out before it is ready, add a little more oil.

3. Meanwhile, rub the bottoms of the *cazuelas* with the garlic clove.

4. Cut the zucchinis into ¼-inch slices.

5. Distribute the onions evenly in the *cazuelas*. Alternate layers of the zucchini on top of the onions, making five rows. Pack the slices in snugly, overlapping them both horizontally and vertically. They will stand up at a slight angle. Sprinkle the thyme leaves on top.

6. Drizzle with the remaining extra-virgin olive oil.

7. Sprinkle with fleur de sel and freshly ground black pepper.

8. Bake for 15 minutes. Remove the *cazuelas* and push down on the vegetables with a metal spatula. Return to the oven and bake until the vegetables are soft and starting to caramelize, about 15 more minutes.

9. Serve directly from the *cazuelas*.

SAVORY APPLE TIANS

4 SERVINGS

4 tablespoons (2 ounces) delicate extra-virgin olive oil, divided

1 large onion (12 ounces), peeled, cut in half, and sliced

fine sea salt

freshly grated nutmeg

4 large apples (about 1½ pounds), peeled, cored, and cut into thin slices

2 teaspoons fresh thyme leaves

fleur de sel and freshly ground black pepper

These tians, apple slices baked atop a bed of onions, make a great side dish with pork chops. Buy crisp, tart apples at a farmers' market if possible. They will be more flavorful than supermarket varieties.

Some extra-virgin olive oils with a high percentage of the Leccino variety have spicy cinnamon notes that would lend special flavor to this dish. Lacking such an oil, use a delicate extra-virgin olive oil.

1. Preheat the oven to 400°F.

2. Heat 2 tablespoons of the extra-virgin olive oil in a medium skillet over medium heat until it trembles, becomes aromatic, and easily coats the bottom of the skillet. Add the onion, sprinkle with salt, and cook over medium heat until it is soft and lightly colored, about 20 minutes. If the onion starts to dry out before it is ready, add a little more oil.

3. Distribute the onions evenly in the *cazuelas*. Lightly grate nutmeg over them.

4. Arrange the apple slices on top of the onions. Pack them in snugly, overlapping the slices both horizontally and vertically. They will stand up at a slight angle. You may not need all the apples.

5. Drizzle the remaining extra-virgin olive oil on top of the apples.

6. Sprinkle with the thyme leaves, fleur de sel, and a few grindings of pepper.

7. Bake for 10 minutes. Remove the *cazuelas* and push down on the apples with a metal spatula. Return to the oven and bake until the apples are tender and lightly browned, about 10 more minutes.

8. Serve directly from the *cazuelas*.

EGGPLANT BAKED WITH EGGS

4 TO 6 SERVINGS

4 tablespoons (2 ounces) medium extra-virgin olive oil, divided

1 leek, washed, green top removed, and sliced into thin rounds

2 garlic cloves, peeled and thinly sliced

fine sea salt and freshly ground black pepper

1/4 cup (2 ounces) dry white wine

One 28-ounce can whole peeled Italian San Marzano tomatoes and their juice

1 eggplant (about 1 pound), peeled and cut into 1/4-inch slices

5 ounces fresh mozzarella cheese, thinly sliced

4 extra-large eggs

I am always looking for new ways to cook eggplant, one of my favorite vegetables. Perusing Waverley Root's *The Food of France* one afternoon, I happened upon a description of this dish in his chapter on Provence. It is the ultimate comfort food—not elaborate, but carefully prepared and perhaps reminiscent of a simple dish from childhood. It makes a satisfying one-dish dinner.

I specify a medium extra-virgin olive oil, but the acidity of tomatoes varies. A delicate, buttery oil will offset tomatoes with pronounced acidity. Taste the tomatoes, then decide which oil to use.

1. Heat 2 tablespoons of the extra-virgin olive oil in a medium saucepan over medium heat until it trembles, becomes aromatic, and easily coats the bottom of the pan. Add the leek and garlic, then sprinkle with salt and pepper. Turn the heat to medium-low, cover the pan, and cook until the vegetables are soft but not browned, about 10 minutes. Add the wine and bring to a simmer. Add the tomatoes and their juice and break them up with a potato masher. Partially cover the pan and simmer over medium heat for 20 minutes. This sauce can be made ahead and then reheated before you assemble the dish.

2. Preheat the oven to 400°F and line a baking pan with parchment paper.

3. Toss the slices of eggplant with the remaining extra-virgin olive oil. Arrange the slices in a single layer on the baking pan. Sprinkle them with salt and pepper. Roast until lightly browned and tender, 10 to 15 minutes.

4. Put the tomato sauce in a 12-by-9-inch gratin dish or baking pan. (If you have made the sauce ahead, reheat it in the gratin dish.) Arrange the roasted eggplant in one layer over the sauce. Top the eggplant with slices of cheese. Bake until the cheese is starting to melt and the sauce in the center of the dish is bubbling, 8 to 10 minutes. Put the eggs in a small bowl and beat them with a fork. Pour the eggs over the cheese and eggplant. Sprinkle salt and pepper over the eggs. Return to the oven and bake until the eggs are set, browned, and slightly puffed, 5 to 8 minutes. Serve immediately.

CANNELLINI BEANS WITH SAUTÉED PUMPKIN CUBES AND OLIO NUOVO

1 cup (7 ounces by weight) dried cannellini beans

slice of onion

1/2 small carrot

1/2 stalk celery

bay leaf

fine sea salt

2 cups (about 10 ounces by weight) fresh pumpkin cut into 1-inch dice

1 teaspoon Aleppo pepper

3 tablespoons (1 1/2 ounces) medium extra-virgin olive oil, divided

freshly ground black pepper

about 3 tablespoons *olio nuovo* for drizzling

This autumn dish celebrates pumpkins and fresh new olive oil on a base of cannellini beans. When buying plants for my garden one year, I couldn't resist a *rouge vif d'etampes* pumpkin, a squat French variety with deep orange skin and flesh, even though I knew that pumpkin plants need a lot of room. I planted it in a raised bed with two tomatoes and eggplants—not nearly enough space. It sent out long shoots like octopus arms, climbing over the other plants. After returning from a vacation, I found that it had left the confines of the bed, crossed a path, and was entangled in the roses. I cut off the longest parts and continued to trim it the rest of the summer, knowing that I was sacrificing most of the fruit. Only one pumpkin survived the pruning—and grew to thirty-six pounds!

I made a several-course pumpkin dinner and served this recipe as a starter. If you don't have a source for these special pumpkins, sugar pumpkins or butternut squash would be worthy substitutes.

The beans must soak overnight, so plan ahead before making this.

1. The evening before you plan to make the dish, put the beans in a bowl, add cold water to cover them by 3 inches, and leave them at room temperature overnight.

2. The next day, drain the beans, put them in a medium saucepan, cover them with 2 inches of cold water, and bring to a simmer. Skim off the foam that rises to the top and add the onion, carrot, celery, and bay leaf. Simmer, partially covered, until the beans are tender, about 1 hour. The cooking time may vary with the age of the beans. Salt the cooking liquid to taste, at least 1 teaspoon.

3. Remove the pan from the heat and let the beans cool to room temperature. Just before cooking the pumpkin, drain the beans and put them in a bowl.

4. Toss the pumpkin cubes with the Aleppo pepper, salt, and 1 tablespoon of medium extra-virgin olive oil.

5. Heat the remaining 2 tablespoons of medium extra-virgin olive oil in a large skillet until it trembles, becomes aromatic, and easily coats the bottom of the skillet. Add the pumpkin and sauté, turning frequently, until all sides are browned and the cubes are tender, about 5 minutes.

6. Mix the pumpkin with the beans. Season with pepper. Drizzle *olio nuovo* over the top before serving.

MUJADDARA

6 tablespoons (3 ounces) medium or robust extra-virgin olive oil, divided

2 medium onions (about 1 pound), peeled and thinly sliced, plus 3 tablespoons finely chopped onions

fine sea salt

1/3 cup (2 1/3 ounces by weight) basmati rice

1 1/3 cups (10 2/3 ounces) water, divided

2/3 cup (4 3/4 ounces by weight) French green lentils

1/4 teaspoon ground cumin

There is a small grocery store called Bi-Rite Market not far from where I live that fell into disrepair some years ago but was resurrected by the offspring of the original owners, a family with Middle Eastern roots. They produce many excellent prepared foods in their cramped kitchen, and my first taste of *mujaddara* was from this store. I often eat this for a simple lunch.

In her novel *Crescent*, Diana Abu-Jaber calls this the ultimate Arab comfort food, with the elemental ingredients of lentils, rice, and onions—she even includes a recipe.

Serve it as a side vegetable dish or part of an antipasto dish.

1. Heat 1/4 cup of the extra-virgin olive oil in a large skillet over high heat until it trembles, becomes aromatic, and easily coats the bottom of the skillet. Add the sliced onions and turn the heat to very low. Sprinkle with salt. Cook the onions uncovered, stirring occasionally, until they are the color of a polished mahogany table, about 1 hour. They will shrink dramatically. Remove the onions from the pan and set them aside.

2. While the onions are cooking, wash the rice in 4 or 5 changes of cold water, then soak it in 2/3 cup water for 30 minutes. Drain, reserving the water.

3. Also while the onions are cooking put the lentils in a medium saucepan and cover them with cold water by 1 inch. Sprinkle with 1/4 teaspoon salt and bring to a simmer. Cover the pan and cook over low heat for 10 minutes—they will not be completely cooked. Remove from heat and drain any excess water. Transfer the lentils to a bowl.

4. Return the saucepan to the stove and heat the remaining 2 tablespoons of extra-virgin olive oil over high heat until it trembles, becomes aromatic, and easily coats the bottom of the pan. Add the chopped onions, lower the heat to medium, and cook until they soften but are not yet brown, about 5 minutes.

5. Add the partially cooked lentils, the rice, the reserved rice water plus enough extra water to make 1⅓ cups total, the ground cumin, and ¼ teaspoon of salt. Bring to a simmer, reduce the heat to low, cover tightly, and cook until the rice and lentils are tender, 10 to 15 minutes. Remove from the heat, uncover, and cool to room temperature.

6. Mix the caramelized onions and their cooking oil into the rice and lentils with a fork.

7. If not serving immediately, transfer to a container and refrigerate for up to a week. Bring to room temperature before serving.

BERKELEY OLIVE GROVE

7 Rocky Drive
Oroville, California 95965
530 533 1814
www.berkeleyolivegrove.com

Between 1913 and 1917, fifteen professors at the University of California at Berkeley and the University of Nevada at Reno, along with other investors, bought acreage at the foot of Table Mountain just north of Oroville. They saw the purchase as an investment for their retirement; in time, some built cottages and lived there when they left the universities.

B. B. Meek and H. S. Johns had subdivided the land into eight- and ten-acre parcels in 1910. Meek saw it as a good spot for olive trees. Olives were in the news: Freda Ehmann had a thriving business canning olives, and much was being written about olive-tree cultivation and oil pressing. The professors came from a variety of disciplines, but not one was in agriculture. Before buying the land, some of them traveled to Italy and Spain to investigate the feasibility of their plan.

Since their expertise was not olive cultivation, they hired a manager for the orchards. His tenure was short; when he failed to show up one day, Dell Chaffin, a University of California agriculture graduate, took over. Today, his descendants still live on and farm acreage just north of the original parcel.

The professors invested well. The trees, all Mission, thrived. Some olives were processed and canned; others were pressed into oil in a mill built by Chaffin in 1920. Eventually, younger generations inherited the properties. By 1993, Dayn Patterson, a descendant of Peter Frandsen, one of the original owners, owned most of the original tract.

Darro Grieco bought the land in 2004 with his wife, Olivia Newsome-Grieco. Like the professors, they didn't know much about olive cultivation. Darro Grieco, with a background in real estate, initially thought to build Italian-style villas. But he came to appreciate the historic nature of the land, and now he is committed to saving the orchard. Under the name the Berkeley Olive Association Historic District, the land is in the National Register of Historic Places for its development of the ripe olive industry, as the largest planting of Mission olives in the area, and as a surviving example of early olive culture in California.

In an effort to refurbish the orchard, Darro consulted with Tuscan olive oil expert Marco Mugelli, who sent an associate from Italy to prune the overgrown trees. Darro worked to get the orchard certified as organic and plans to add an irrigation system to the dry-farmed trees.

A year after buying the orchard, it yielded 326 tons of olives for the Griecos. Because this was before the trees were pruned, workers used ladders to reach the fruit and knock it onto tarpaulins on the ground. They sold the crop for pressing. But Darro wants to build a mill, one with a capacity of two or three tons per hour, in an old barn on the property so he can bottle and sell his own oil. Olivia is working on packaging ideas.

Before a tour of the orchard, Darro drove up the mountain so I could see the lay of the land. The tall trees sit in stony loam soil with an old irrigation canal running through them. He pointed out a series of buildings on the north edge of the property, now in disrepair, that housed migrant laborers as late as 1991. On the far side of the orchard, hidden by the trees, is another camp. As housing, the buildings aren't worth saving, but Darro thinks they might be useful for growing mushrooms, maybe even a strawberry nursery.

Although the camp buildings have little value as housing, Olivia has remodeling plans for other structures, including two small stone cottages that stand at the entrance to the property. After a commercial kitchen is installed, she sees them as a venue for weddings and an agriturismo.

The Griecos are only at the beginning of their project, but they are clearly committed to producing the best olive oil that the trees can make. "When we first bought the property, Olivia and I called our land Terra Fortunata, fortunate land, but really, we are the fortunate ones."

DAVERO

766 Westside Road
Healdsburg, California 95448
707 433 2345
www.davero.com

The single-lane road eventually gave way to a clearing, and I saw a comfortable country home on the other side of a pond. The driveway curved past a grove of seventy-five Meyer lemon trees, the source for the lemon oil that DaVero makes, and stopped at the "shipping department," a large shed filled with jams from estate-grown fruit, vinegar custom made and bottled for DaVero, honey from hives on the property, and of course olive oil. Colleen Mc-Glynn, the owner of DaVero with her husband, Ridgely Evers, welcomed me and hushed the dog, who was barking a greeting.

Ridgely bought the ranch in 1982 and, after renovating the house, thought about uses for the rest of the land. He wanted to grow something but wasn't excited about grapes. Like others in the renaissance of California olive oil, he went to Tuscany and was lured into the olive world. He especially liked the oil made by Fattoria Bernardini in the Lucca area and decided to import the same mix of trees—Frantoio, Leccino, Pendolino, and Maurino—directly from them. But what should have been a straightforward transaction got complicated. The trees were booked on a flight from Milan to San Francisco through Frankfurt on Lufthansa. Instead, someone in Italy decided that Italian trees should travel on an Italian airline, so the trees were sent directly from Milan to Los Angeles via Alitalia. Since San Francisco and Los Angeles are both in California, the Italian official may have concluded that they weren't far apart. While Ridgely was tapping his foot awaiting the trees' arrival in Northern California, custom officials in Los Angeles were considering destroying the entire lot because of dirt (which was actually sterile peat moss and perlite) on the roots. Foreign soil is not allowed into the country. When customs notified Ridgely, he persuaded two friends to go to the airport and cleanse the trees, all 2,400 of them. They finally made it north and were put into pots until they could be planted. A month later there was a major freeze; one third of the trees were lost. Finally the survivors were in the ground in 1991.

Many of the 4,500 trees now growing were cuttings of this original batch. The DaVero Dry Creek Estate Extra-Virgin Olive Oil is made in the same style as the Bernardini oil, a mix of 50 percent Leccino, 25 percent Frantoio, 15 percent Maurino, and 10 percent Pendolino.

Ridgely and Colleen harvested the first olives in 1994, one ton of fruit that produced twenty-five gallons of oil. The next year was more plentiful—the trees produced enough olives to press a hundred gallons. In 2008, they expect about fourteen hundred gallons of extra-virgin oil and five hundred gallons of Meyer lemon oil.

The first olives were pressed in the Central Valley, then for ten years they trucked the fruit to Roberto Zecca's Frantoio, a unique space that is both a restaurant and olive press, in Mill Valley. Now they drive them north to Olivino's hammer mill in Hopland. During the harvest the workers hand pick the fruit, sometimes using handheld shakers to knock the fruit onto tarpaulins on the ground, sometimes climbing trees. They pick two or three tons a day, then leave for the mill at about four P.M.

The finished oil is stored in nearby Geyserville in stainless-steel tanks that are topped with inert gas, then transferred to smaller tanks and sent to a bottler as needed.

In the early years, Ridgely and Colleen were the sales force, going to restaurants and retail stores, often holding tastings to introduce customers to their wares. Colleen did lots of what she called "missionary work" in grocery stores. People unfamiliar with good olive oil often thought the price was steep. "Even though they might be drinking two ounces of expensive wheat juice that was gone in a few minutes," she told me.

They tried a distributor for a while but realized that his percentage, as well as the low wholesale price, was cutting into their already low profit margin. Now they sell through their web site, in their retail store, and to chefs and restaurants. Mario Batali uses their oil in his New York restaurants and on his popular television show. Each time he wields a bottle of their oil in front of the camera, there is a blip in sales.

Like some other small-scale producers in California, Ridgely still works another job. A long-time entrepreneur in the computer business, he was absent the day of my visit, off in Southern California on a business trip as founder and CEO of NetBooks—whatever it takes to keep the olive oil flowing.

DOUGHS AND PASTAS

When I had a bakery, we made *fougasse*s cut into tree shapes and flavored with garlic and fresh rosemary. We also made regular loaves from the same dough and called them fougasse loaves, somewhat of a misnomer. They were one of our most popular breads. Italy's focaccie are a variation on the same theme.

Pizzas, simple in concept, deserve good extra-virgin olive oil, especially for the final finish when they come out of the oven.

There is only one pasta recipe in this chapter, but it is an essential one. The reason for its existence is to welcome the latest harvest of *olio nuovo*.

Pizza Dough

Pizza makers in Naples take their jobs seriously. Government regulations specify exactly how authentic *pizza Napoletana* must be made. The rules include such things as type of oven (wood-fired), kneading times for the dough (twenty minutes), and the thickness of the dough after shaping (0.11 inch in the middle and 0.4 to 0.8 inch at the borders). The flour used is type 00, similar to our all-purpose flour, but not quite the same. Although it may be equal in protein content, it is milled finer, so it has a more powdery texture. However, when baked, doughs made with the two flours are more similar than different. Because type 00 is available here (I have even seen it in bulk at a health-food store), I include a recipe using it.

These recipes include a technique borrowed from the French called *autolyse*. (The recipes for Focaccie, Pissaladière, and Sweet Fougasses also include this method.) After the dough is mixed briefly, it rests for twenty minutes. This lets the flour absorb the liquid so the final kneading time is much less. Although the French don't add salt until the final kneading, I see no harm in adding it at the beginning.

Letting the pizza dough rise overnight in the refrigerator develops more flavor, so plan to make it the day before you bake.

Pizzas need a hot oven. A home baker cannot achieve the heat that commercial pizza makers do, but using a baking stone and preheating the oven for forty-five minutes at its highest thermostat setting gives a close approximation.

Of course, a drizzle of extra-virgin olive oil before and often after baking is essential.

7. Slide the pizza onto the baking stone using a quick into-the-oven-and-out motion. If your oven is large enough, bake two pizzas at a time. If you are making more pizzas than your oven can accommodate, cover the remaining dough with a kitchen towel until there is oven space. Bake until the crust is brown and the toppings are bubbling, about 10 minutes. Put the tip of the peel under a pizza and use the same quick into-the-oven motion to get it onto the peel, then remove it from the oven.

8. Cut into wedges and serve at once.

VARIATION:
PIZZA DOUGH WITH AMERICAN FLOUR

Because American all-purpose flour has more spring, this recipe includes a little extra-virgin olive oil to tenderize it.

1. Follow the directions for Neapolitan-style pizza dough using 1²/₃ cups (13 ounces) warm water plus 2 tablespoons (1 ounce) delicate extra-virgin olive oil instead of 1¾ cups water. Use unbleached all-purpose flour instead of 00 flour.

Pizza Toppings

There are endless combinations, many not traditional, to use for pizza toppings. Right now pizza is the rage in San Francisco, so much so that the *San Francisco Chronicle* includes brief reviews of pizza places in each week's food section. Cheese isn't mandatory, although *quattro formaggi* is still popular. Seasonal ingredients shine, and sometimes uncooked salad greens are added as the pizzas come out of the oven. Use your imagination, but keep the amount of toppings in check so the dough isn't smothered.

Here are a some suggestions; each will top one 10-inch pizza.

OYSTER MUSHROOMS AND TOMME DE SAVOIE

2 ounces oyster mushrooms, brushed clean and torn into large pieces

2 ounces Tomme de Savoie cheese cut into ½-inch dice

fine sea salt and freshly ground black pepper

2 tablespoons (1 ounce) delicate extra-virgin olive oil, divided

1. Strew the mushrooms over the stretched dough, leaving an uncovered border around the edge. Top with the cheese. Salt lightly and add a few grindings of pepper. Drizzle with 1 table-spoon of the olive oil, being careful to moisten the uncovered border. Bake until browned and bubbling. Remove from the oven and drizzle with the remaining 1 tablespoon of olive oil.

BRUSSELS SPROUTS WITH SHALLOTS AND PECORINO ROMANO

5 Brussels sprouts (about 3 ounces), halved and cut into 1/16-inch slices

1 tablespoon minced shallot

3 tablespoons (1 1/2 ounces) robust extra-virgin olive oil, divided

4 tablespoons grated Pecorino Romano

fine sea salt and freshly ground black pepper

1. Toss the Brussels sprouts and shallot with 2 tablespoons of the olive oil. Put them on the stretched dough, leaving an uncovered border around the edge. Spread the cheese on top. Sprinkle with salt and a few grindings of pepper. Drizzle a little of the remaining olive oil on the uncovered border. Bake until browned and bubbling. Moisten with the rest of the olive oil before serving.

TOMATO AND SORREL

10 large sorrel leaves, ribs removed, cut into julienne

2 medium vine-ripened tomatoes, preferably heirloom, cut into 1/4-inch slices

fine sea salt and freshly ground black pepper

3 tablespoons (1 1/2 ounces) delicate or medium extra-virgin olive oil, divided

1. Strew the julienned sorrel on the stretched dough, leaving an uncovered border around the edge. Arrange the tomatoes in a single layer on top of the sorrel. Add salt and pepper. Drizzle with half of the olive oil, being careful to moisten the uncovered border. Bake until browned and bubbling. Drizzle with the remaining oil before serving.

NOTE: For a variation on this topping, use fresh basil leaves instead of sorrel and drizzle with basil olive oil.

EGGPLANT WITH MINT

1 eggplant, about 1 pound, peeled and cut into ¼-inch slices, then 1½-inch strips

3 tablespoons (1½ ounces) medium extra-virgin olive oil, divided

handful fresh mint leaves (about ½ cup)

fine sea salt and freshly ground black pepper

1. Preheat the oven to 400°F and line a baking pan with parchment paper.

2. Put the eggplant in a bowl and toss it with 1 tablespoon of the oil. Sprinkle with salt and a few grindings of pepper. Arrange the slices in a single layer on the baking pan. Roast in the oven until lightly browned and tender, 10 to 15 minutes. Cool to room temperature. (This can be done ahead.)

3. When you are ready to make the pizza, strew the mint leaves over the stretched dough, leaving an uncovered border around the edge. Top with the eggplant strips. Drizzle the remaining 2 tablespoons of oil on top, being careful to moisten the uncovered border. Bake until browned and bubbling.

NOTE: If you live near a farmers' market or Asian grocery store where Thai and Vietnamese herbs are available, substitute Thai basil leaves (*rau que*) and rice paddy herb (*ngo om*) for the mint.

POTATOES WITH ONIONS AND BLUE CHEESE

1/2 medium onion, very thinly sliced

1 medium waxy unpeeled potato or 2 fingerlings, cut into 1/16-inch slices, preferably on a mandoline

fine sea salt and freshly ground black pepper

2 ounces blue cheese (your favorite type), cut into 1/2-inch pieces

2 tablespoons (1 ounce) delicate extra-virgin olive oil

1. Put the onion slices on the stretched dough, leaving an uncovered border around the edge. Top with a single layer of potato slices placed close together. Season with salt and pepper. Dab the cheese on top. Drizzle with the olive oil, being careful to moisten the uncovered border. Bake until browned and bubbling.

Focaccie

These yeasted flatbreads, seasoned with herbs or cheese, are found throughout Italy. They also appear in the south of France, where they are called *fougasses* and are made into fanciful shapes such as trees or ladders. Serve them with meals or use them to make sandwiches. Try the Focaccia with Scallions and Rosemary variation to make Pan Bagnat (see recipe, p. 53).

Use a medium or robust extra-virgin olive oil.

FOCACCIA WITH PUMPKIN SEEDS AND THYME

2 RECTANGULAR, 6-BY-10-INCH FLATBREADS

1²/₃ cups (13 ounces) warm water, plus more if needed

2¹/₄ teaspoons active dry yeast

6 tablespoons (3 ounces) medium or robust extra-virgin olive oil

¹/₃ cup (1³/₄ ounces by weight) whole hulled pumpkin seeds

1 tablespoon fresh thyme leaves

4¹/₂ cups (1 pound, 7 ounces by weight) unbleached all-purpose flour

2¹/₂ teaspoons fine sea salt

One of my favorite bakeries, Della Fattoria, makes loaves of bread studded with pumpkin seeds. It was an inspiration for this focaccia.

1. Pour the water into the bowl of a stand mixer. Sprinkle on the yeast and wait until it dissolves and becomes creamy, about 3 minutes. Add the olive oil, pumpkin seeds, and thyme. Stir the the flour and salt together and add them to the bowl. Using a dough hook, mix on slow speed until the flour is absorbed. Drizzle in a little more water as needed to moisten any flour at the bottom of the bowl. Mix just until the dough comes together, about 2 minutes. It will still look rough and shaggy.

2. Turn off the mixer and let the dough rest for 20 minutes. Restart the mixer and knead on medium speed until the dough forms a ball and is elastic, about 3 minutes.

3. Remove the bowl from the mixer, remove the dough hook, and cover the bowl with plastic wrap. Leave at room temperature until the dough doubles, 2½ to 3 hours.

4. Line a 12-by-18-by-1-inch baking pan with parchment paper.

5. Turn the dough out onto a lightly floured work surface. Divide it into halves. Shape each half into a rectangle. Cover with a kitchen towel and let the rectangles rest for 10 minutes. Patting and pushing with your hands, enlarge each rectangle to 6 by 10 inches. Put the rectangles on the baking pan. Slide the pan into a large plastic bag, shake the top a few times to introduce air so the bag won't stick to the dough, and tie the ends closed. Leave at room temperature until the dough doubles, about 1½ hours.

6. Position racks on the lowest level and in the middle of the oven. Place an empty baking pan on the lower rack. Put a baking stone on the middle rack. Preheat the oven to 425°F for 45 minutes.

7. When the dough is ready, bring 1½ cups of water to a boil.

8. Remove the baking pan from the plastic bag. Cut away the parchment paper close to the risen dough. Transfer one rectangle, still on the parchment paper, onto a peel or rimless baking sheet. Using your fingertips, dimple the surface of the dough.

9. Slide the rectangle onto the baking stone using a quick into-the-oven-and-out motion. Repeat with the other rectangle.

10. Wearing oven mitts, immediately pour the boiling water into the empty pan in the bottom of the oven and close the door. Be careful—this will cause an immediate burst of steam.

11. Bake until the breads are browned and sound hollow when thumped on the bottom, about 30 minutes. Put the tip of the peel under a loaf and use the same quick into-the-oven motion to get the bread onto the peel, then remove it from the oven. Repeat with the other loaf.

12. Remove the parchment paper and cool the breads on a rack.

FOCACCIA WITH PANCETTA

5 ounces pancetta, cut into ½-inch dice

The pancetta flavor really permeates this bread. Toast slices and serve with poached eggs for breakfast instead of bacon and eggs.

1. Heat a medium skillet over high heat. When a drop of water dances on the surface, add the pancetta pieces and reduce the heat to medium. Cook, turning them occasionally, until they are brown all over, 15 to 20 minutes. Drain the meat on paper towels.

2. Follow the instructions in the focaccia recipe, adding the cooked pancetta to the water and oil instead of the pumpkin seeds and thyme.

FOCACCIA WITH SCALLIONS AND ROSEMARY

3 scallions, green tops removed, thinly sliced

2 tablespoons finely chopped fresh rosemary

At my bakery we made a *fougasse* with garlic and rosemary. This is a less assertive version of that bread.

1. Heat the 6 tablespoons olive oil over medium heat in a small saucepan until it trembles, becomes aromatic, and easily coats the bottom of the pan. Add the scallions and rosemary and simmer until the scallions start to become translucent, about 1½ minutes. Remove from the heat and cool to room temperature.

2. Follow the directions in the focaccia recipe, adding the infused oil and the cooked scallions after the yeast becomes creamy and omitting the pumpkin seeds and thyme.

PISSALADIÈRE

ONE 12-INCH PISSALADIÈRE

²/₃ cup (5¼ ounces) whole milk, warmed to room temperature, plus more if needed

1½ teaspoons active dry yeast

5 tablespoons (2½ ounces) delicate, somewhat sweet extra-virgin olive oil

1 extra-large egg, at room temperature

3 cups (15 ounces by weight) unbleached all-purpose flour

1¾ teaspoons fine sea salt

5 tablespoons (2½ ounces) medium or robust extra-virgin olive oil

3 medium onions (about 1½ pounds), peeled, halved, and thinly sliced

freshly ground black pepper

2 teaspoons fresh thyme leaves

fine white cornmeal for the peel

8 anchovy filets, either packed in olive oil or *crudo* packed in salt (see recipe, p. 123), rinsed, patted dry, and coarsely chopped

15 whole black Niçoise-style olives, pitted

This Provençal flatbread is much like a pizza, but with a well-defined topping of cooked onions, anchovies, and Niçoise olives—no cheese. In *English Bread and Yeast Cookery*, Elizabeth David explains that the name is derived from *pissala*, a fish paste made from immature anchovies and sardines, once plentiful off the coast of Nice but now illegal to fish. By the 1930s larger anchovies had replaced the paste, but the name of the dish remained.

The dough, a variation of Elizabeth David's recipe, resembles a cross between a pizza dough and a brioche-style dough made with extra-virgin olive oil rather than butter.

1. To make the dough, put the milk in the bowl of a stand mixer. Sprinkle the yeast over it and wait until the yeast dissolves, about 3 minutes. Add the delicate olive oil and the egg. Stir the flour and 1¾ teaspoons salt together and add them to the bowl. Using a dough hook, mix on slow speed until the flour is absorbed. Drizzle in a little more milk as needed to moisten any flour at the bottom of the bowl. Mix just until the dough comes together, about 2 minutes. It will still look rough and shaggy.

2. Turn off the mixer and let the dough rest for 20 minutes. Restart the mixer and knead on medium speed until the dough forms a ball and is elastic, about 3 minutes.

3. Remove the dough hook. Cover the mixer bowl with plastic wrap and leave at room temperature until the dough doubles, 2½ to 3 hours.

4. While the dough is rising, heat 4 tablespoons of the more robust olive oil in a medium skillet over medium heat until it trembles, becomes aromatic, and easily coats the bottom of the pan. Add the onions and sprinkle them with salt. Cook the onions, stirring occasionally, until they brown and just start to caramelize, about 30 minutes. Add more salt and pepper to taste. Add the thyme. Remove from the pan and cool to room temperature.

5. Preheat the oven to 450˚F for 45 minutes with a baking stone on the middle shelf.

6. Turn the dough out onto a lightly floured work surface and shape it into a round. Cover with a kitchen towel and let it rest for 5 minutes. Then, using your hands and a rolling pin, shape the dough into a 12-inch round about ¼ inch thick.

7. Transfer the dough to a peel or a rimless baking sheet dusted with cornmeal. Mix the anchovies with the onions and put them on the dough, leaving a ½-inch border exposed around the edge. Drizzle the remaining tablespoon of extra-virgin olive oil on the exposed dough.

8. Slide the pissaladière onto the baking stone using a quick into-the-oven-and-out motion. Bake until the crust is brown, about 15 minutes. Put the tip of the peel under the pissaladière and use the same quick into-the-oven motion to slide it onto the peel, then remove it from the oven.

9. Transfer it onto a cutting surface and top with the olives. Cut into wedges and serve.

SPAGHETTI WITH OLIO NUOVO

4 TO 6 SERVINGS

1 pound dried spaghetti, preferably Italian

6 tablespoons (3 ounces) *olio nuovo*, divided

6 large garlic cloves, peeled and sliced

1/4 teaspoon dried red chile flakes

fleur de sel

Steven Dambeck of Apollo Olive Oil (see p. 66) described the first oil he made using Marco Mugelli's vacuum system in a piece he wrote for *Edible Sacramento*. Everyone was nervous as the oil flowed from the decanter. Would this special system produce great oil? One by one, the millers held tasting cups under the spout, collected the green oil, and tasted. But they were really interested in Marco's opinion. He took his time filling a cup, swirled the oil to appreciate its aroma, then tipped it to his lips, sucking in air. After he swallowed, he said, "Tonight we eat spaghetti with garlic, oil, and red pepper." They were magical words to Steven—their oil was worthy of this simple Italian dish that celebrates the new olive oil of the year.

Use an *olio nuovo* and serve with a crisp green salad.

1. Bring about 5 quarts of generously salted water to a boil in a large pot. Add the spaghetti and cook until al dente, about 12 minutes.

2. While the pasta is cooking, heat 2 tablespoons of the olive oil in a small pot over medium heat until it trembles, becomes aromatic, and easily coats the bottom of the pan. Add the garlic and cook until lightly browned, about 1 minute. Add the red chile flakes and turn off the heat.

3. Drain the pasta. Add the oil with the garlic and pepper, the remaining 4 tablespoons of oil, and a sprinkling of fleur de sel. Toss until all the strands of pasta glisten.

4. Serve in hot bowls.

STELLA CADENTE OLIVE OIL

P.O. Box 37
Palermo, California 95968
800 305 1288
www.stellacadente.com

A sounder of wild boars walked through a broken gate and uprooted the first two hundred olive trees that Sue Ellery and Tom Hunter planted in 1995. Undaunted, the fledging olive orchardists fixed the gate and replanted, this time four hundred trees. The planting held, despite some loss from frost, rabbits, and gophers. Now close to thirteen hundred trees grow on seven acres of gentle hills surrounding their home in Northern California's Anderson Valley.

The couple didn't start out as farmers. Both worked in high-tech companies in the San Francisco Bay Area before they purchased the land in Boonville. Sue traveled to the ranch on weekends and, remembering the beauty of the olive groves she saw in Italy during trips as a child, dreamed of planting her own. A horticulturalist friend tried to discourage her; in his opinion the trees wouldn't thrive. But she persisted, reasoning that if Chardonnay and Pinot Noir grapes grew in the valley, olives should too. To learn

more, the couple joined the California Olive Oil Council in 1994 and went on tours of successful olive orchards. They also took classes on olive tree cultivation from the University of California Cooperative Extension, as well as an olive oil sensory evaluation course.

They purchased their first trees from McEvoy Ranch, a pioneer in the renaissance of olive oil in California. The trees had Italian ancestry—Frantoio, Leccino, Pendolino, and Coratina. By 2000 they had enough fruit for a harvest. They stripped the olives from the branches and took them to the Olive Press, a small operation in nearby Sonoma Valley. The pressing yielded a modest production that they sold at the homey Boonville farmers' market on Saturday mornings.

By 2001 both had left their urban jobs and moved to the country to immerse themselves in olive oil. Within a few years, the demand for their oil exceeded the crop. To fill it out, they bought

Mission olives from a grower in Oroville, to the northeast, where olives have been grown, mostly for canning, for years. Now they have a partner in Oroville who grows four hundred acres of Mission olives. In addition to mixing some with their small Tuscan production, they mill them with citrus, either Meyer lemons, blood oranges, or Persian limes, to make infused oils. The newest is an oil milled with fresh basil that calls out for a plate of juicy tomatoes. These infused oils are very popular; the Meyer lemon is their best seller.

They sell their oil in twenty-one states, mostly in specialty shops and gourmet markets. They also have three olive oil bars, areas in stores where customers can taste oil and buy in bulk, and they plan to open more.

The couple haven't neglected their original plantings; this harvest is now processed on McEvoy's state-of-the-art equipment. The danger of frost dictates an early harvest, which can tip the scale toward bitterness and pungency, but their aim is to produce a milder oil, easier on the American palate. In 2006 they nailed it. Their Tuscan blend won a best of class gold medal at the Los Angeles County Fair.

THE OLIVE PRESS
MAKERS & PURVEYORS OF AWARD-WINNING OLIVE OIL

THE OLIVE PRESS

24724 Arnold Drive
Sonoma, California 95476
800 965 4839
www.theolivepress.com

Deborah Rogers, co-owner of the Olive Press with Ed Stolman, is widely respected for her prowess at milling olives and for her fine-tuned palate. She is a longtime member of the California Olive Oil Council and the University of California research taste panels, and people new to the milling business often seek her advice. But before 1993 these skills were waiting to emerge. A horticulture degree and a love of growing and cooking drove her desire to plant olive trees on a five-acre parcel of land she and her husband bought in the hamlet of Glen Ellen, California. To better immerse herself in the olive world, she went to an olive festival put on by B. C. Cohn, one of the growers of the newly awakened olive oil movement, in 1994. There she realized that she didn't have to wait five years for new trees to bear fruit before she got into the olive oil business. At B. C. Cohn's second festival, she arrived with Italian bottles filled to the very top (too full, really—in the heat of the day the corks popped out) with a blend she had made from two drums of olive oil she had purchased on the bulk market. She sold them all.

By this time, she had met others interested in olive oil, including Paul Vossen, Ed Stolman, Lila Jaeger, and Ridgely Evers. A group of thirty, led by Paul, went on a tour of olive producers and millers in the south of France. Many of the mills were old, and Deborah calls this trip the defining moment—she finally understood what fusty was.

Another member of the group, Ed Stolman, had a vision when he got home. A successful businessman, he retired, moved to Glen Ellen in the early 1990s, and planted olive trees imported from Italy. He decided to build an olive press and persuaded some of his fellow travelers from the French trip to become investors. Deborah Rogers wrote a check.

Meanwhile, she continued to blend and sell bulk oil. She teamed up with V. G. Buck, another seller of bulk oil. First they sold at farmers' markets, then throughout the San Francisco Bay Area, then nationally. Their oil was the first to be placed in Safeway stores. Keeping the business afloat was a struggle, and eventually Napa Valley Kitchens bought their company. She stayed on for a while, but really wanted to grow and mill her own olives, so she quit in 2000. She was planning to stay home with her nine-year-old son for the summer, but then she got a phone call from Ed. He wanted her to manage the harvest and milling at his press. She took on the job, even though she had never actually done any milling. By the following January, she was the managing partner of the Olive Press. In 2005, Ed bought out the rest of the partners, so now it's just the two of them.

In addition to custom milling for clients, Deborah mills oils for the Olive Press label. She started with Mission, Sevillano, and Ascolano, the old California varieties, and wants to continue milling them because of their historical importance.

Just before the harvest starts, she is in frequent touch with growers, many of whom are anxious to pick, worried that the olives will get too ripe or a frost might damage them. If she thinks it's too early, she encourages them to wait. And she admonishes those who bring fruit that isn't up to caliber. She doesn't want all green fruit (the resulting oil will be too bitter). And blemished, dirty, olive-fly infested, or moldy olives will mar the oil. "If you bought a peach at a store, you wouldn't buy one that was bruised or moldy. Olives are fruit!"

MEAT AND POULTRY

I've borrowed from several cuisines, with their varied cooking methods and seasonings, for these recipes. Of course, they all depend on extra-virgin olive oil—for cooking, for finishing a dish, or as an integral part of a sauce. There is a dish for every taste here, from a simple grilled steak to a long-braised stew that allows the flavors to mingle.

SLOW-COOKED LAMB SHANKS WITH FLAGEOLET BEANS

4 TO 6 SERVINGS

2 cups (13 ounces by weight) green flageolet beans

4 lamb shanks (4 to 4½ pounds), trimmed of excess fat

fine sea salt and freshly ground black pepper

¼ cup (2 ounces) delicate or medium extra-virgin olive oil, plus more for drizzling over the finished dish

1 large onion, peeled and coarsely chopped

6 garlic cloves, peeled

2 celery stalks, stalks cut into ¼-inch slices and 2 tablespoons roughly chopped leaves

2 medium carrots, peeled and cut into ¼-inch slices

2 teaspoons whole fennel seeds

½ teaspoon ground allspice

¾ cup (6 ounces) dry white wine

about 1½ cups (12 ounces) water

This slow-cooked stew tastes even better if made ahead and reheated because the flavors mingle more. I often cook it in my wood-fired oven at our country house, slipping it in just before bedtime after the oven's temperature has dropped. The oven slowly loses heat as the hours pass—by morning, it is often less than 200 degrees. The first person out of bed in the morning takes the stew out, and we reheat it for lunch or dinner. The portions are ample, enough for four hearty eaters or six less robust diners.

In San Francisco, without my wood-fired oven, I cook it on top of the stove.

Delicate oil makes the meat taste sweeter, but medium oil suits the rustic nature of the dish.

Plan your schedule so you can soak the beans overnight.

1. The evening before you plan to make the dish, put the beans in a bowl, add cold water to cover them by 3 inches, and leave them at room temperature overnight.

2. Season the lamb shanks with salt and pepper. In a heavy casserole that will hold the shanks snugly, heat the ¼ cup extra-virgin olive oil over medium heat until it trembles, becomes aromatic, and easily coats the bottom of the casserole. Brown the shanks, two at a time. Set them aside.

3. Put the onion, garlic, celery, celery leaves, carrots, fennel seeds, and allspice in the casserole. Season the vegetables with salt and pepper. Reduce the heat to medium-low, cover, and cook until the onions are translucent but not brown, about 10 minutes.

4. Add the wine, bring to a brisk simmer, and reduce the liquid by half, uncovered, about 3 minutes. Return the lamb shanks and any accumulated juices to the casserole and bring to a slow simmer. Cover the pan and cook at barely a simmer for 1 hour, adding a little water if the vegetables become dry.

5. Carefully remove the shanks. Drain and rinse the beans and add them to the casserole with 1 teaspoon of salt. Add enough water to just cover the beans, about 1½ cups.

6. Return the shanks to the casserole, turning them over. Bring back to a slow simmer and skim off any foam. Cover and cook at barely a simmer until the beans are soft and the meat is tender and falling off the bone, about 1½ hours.

7. Either spoon the beans onto plates and top each serving with a lamb shank and a drizzle of extra-virgin olive oil or put the shanks on a cutting board, remove the meat from the bones following the natural separations, and return to the casserole. Reheat, then serve, adding a drizzle of extra-virgin olive oil.

LAMB AND BULGUR WHEAT MEATBALLS

24 MEATBALLS, 6 TO 8 FIRST-COURSE SERVINGS, 4 TO 6 MAIN

½ cup (5½ ounces by weight) fine bulgur wheat

10 tablespoons (5 ounces) medium extra-virgin olive oil, divided

1 medium onion (about 8 ounces), peeled and finely chopped

2 garlic cloves, peeled and finely chopped

fine sea salt

1½ teaspoons *za'atar*

½ teaspoon Aleppo pepper

1 extra-large egg, beaten with a fork

1 tablespoon pomegranate molasses

1 pound ground lamb

freshly ground black pepper

2 cups (16 ounces) whole-milk yogurt

2 tablespoons finely chopped parsley

robust extra-virgin olive oil for serving

One year a friend returned from a trip to Israel with a bag of *za'atar* for me. Although I knew the name of this aromatic seasoning, a blend of sesame seeds, thyme, marjoram, and sumac, I had never used it. When rubbed on chicken before grilling, it added an earthy tone, but I think it's even better in these meatballs. You can find it Middle Eastern stores, along with the pomegranate molasses used in this recipe, or you can make your own; Mourad Lahlou, the chef at San Francisco's Aziza restaurant, combines equal parts of the above ingredients, then powders them in a spice grinder.

If fresh pomegranates are in season, sprinkle a few of the seeds on each plate before serving.

1. Put the bulgur in a bowl and add enough cold water to cover it by about 1 inch. Soak for 15 minutes. Line a sieve with cheesecloth. Pour the soaked bulgur into the lined sieve. Gather the bulgur in the cheesecloth and squeeze it dry.

2. Heat 2 tablespoons of the medium extra-virgin olive oil in a medium skillet over medium heat until it trembles, becomes aromatic, and easily coats the bottom of the skillet. Add the onion and garlic and sprinkle with salt. Cover the pan and cook over medium-low heat until the onion is translucent but not brown, about 10 minutes. Add the *za'atar* and Aleppo pepper, increase the heat to medium, and cook another minute. Remove from the heat, transfer to a medium bowl, and cool to room temperature.

3. When the onion has cooled, add the bulgur wheat, egg, pomegranate molasses, and lamb. Sprinkle with 1 teaspoon salt and a few grindings of black pepper.

4. Using your hands, mix everything together, then shape the mixture into meatballs about 1½ inches in diameter and put them on a plate. Refrigerate them for 1 hour.

5. While the meatballs rest, combine the yogurt with the parsley and refrigerate.

6. Preheat the oven to 150°F.

7. Pour the remaining ½ cup of medium extra-virgin olive oil in a small skillet. Heat over medium heat until the oil trembles, becomes aromatic, and easily coats the bottom of the skillet. Add 8 meatballs. Turn the meatballs with tongs as they cook, to color them evenly and preserve their shape. Cook until they are well-browned and firm, 5 to 8 minutes.

8. Drain the cooked meatballs on paper towels and keep them warm in the oven while you continue cooking until all are done.

9. Serve immediately with yogurt and parsley sauce. Pass a cruet of robust extra-virgin olive oil for drizzling.

BRAISED CHICKEN THIGHS WITH SWEET POTATOES, QUINCES, AND CARROTS

6 SERVINGS

6 (about 2¹/₂ pounds) bone-in chicken thighs, trimmed of excess fat and skin

fine sea salt and freshly ground black pepper

3 tablespoons (1¹/₂ ounces) medium extra-virgin olive oil

1 large onion (about 12 ounces), peeled and coarsely chopped

1 tablespoon ground ras el hanout

¹/₂ cup (4 ounces) dry white wine

2 large sweet potatoes (about 1 pound), peeled and cut into 1-inch rounds

2 medium quinces (about 1 pound), peeled and cut from their cores, each into 6 pieces

3 medium carrots (about 8 ounces), peeled and cut into ³/₄-inch slices

Although I have used quinces in desserts for years, I love them in savory dishes too. They have a primitive, earthy flavor that goes as well with meat as in a sweet tart.

Ras el hanout is a blend of spices, sometimes dozens of them, that is used in North African dishes. The literal translation is "head of the shop," and each spice shop concocts its own special blend. When slow-cooked with meat and vegetables, it lends a rich, complex flavor. Grind the mix to a powder just before use in a spice grinder or a coffee mill reserved for spices.

I like the versions from Le Sanctuaire and Goumanyat. See Resources for other sources.

1. Sprinkle the chicken with salt and a few grindings of pepper.

2. Heat the extra-virgin olive oil in a medium casserole or deep iron skillet over medium-high heat until it trembles, becomes aromatic, and easily coats the bottom of the vessel. Brown the thighs 3 at a time, starting skin side down, until golden brown, 3 to 4 minutes per side. Remove from the pan and set aside.

3. Add the onion and ras el hanout. Season with salt and pepper. Reduce the heat to medium-low, cover, and cook until the onion is translucent but not brown, about 10 minutes.

4. Add the wine, bring to a brisk simmer, uncovered, and reduce the liquid by half, about 2 minutes.

5. Return the chicken and any accumulated juices to the pot, cover, and cook over medium-low heat for 15 minutes. Add the sweet potatoes, quinces, and carrots to the pot. Season with salt and pepper. Cover and continue to cook until the vegetables are soft and the chicken is tender, 35 to 40 minutes.

6. Serve on hot plates.

GRILLED GRASS-FED RIB STEAK

2 TO 4 SERVINGS

1 (about 1½ pounds) bone-in grass-fed rib steak, at room temperature

fine sea salt and freshly ground black pepper

3 to 4 tablespoons (1½-2 ounces) robust extra-virgin olive oil

Many people are shunning corn-fed beef from animals raised on feedlots due to concerns about food safety, health, and animal mistreatment, or because they prefer the taste of grass-fed beef. The meat is leaner, so it is best cooked rare.

The inspiration for this recipe came from a steak my husband ordered at the restaurant Globe in San Francisco. It was from a small ranch in Northern California and came to the table sliced from the bone, glistening with extra-virgin olive oil. Luckily, he let me taste it.

This recipe, which may seem bare-bones, exemplifies the best approach to stellar ingredients: Keep it simple and manipulate them as little as possible.

A robust extra-virgin olive oil holds its own against the intensity of the meat. Another choice of condiment would be Green Sauce (see recipe, p. 86).

1. Generously season the meat with salt and pepper.

2. Prepare a hardwood charcoal fire and grill the steak over it. The cooking time will depend on the steak's thickness. A steak 1¾ inches thick will take about 6 minutes per side. You can check the temperature with an instant-read thermometer; it should be 120°F. (The temperature will rise about 5 degrees while it rests.)

3. Remove the steak from the grill. Cover it loosely with foil and let it rest at room temperature for 10 minutes.

4. Cut it into slices and arrange on warm plates. Generously drizzle with extra-virgin olive oil.

PAELLA WITH RABBIT AND GREEN BEANS

8 SERVINGS

3/4 cup (5 ounces by weight) small dried white beans

1/3 cup (2²/3 ounces) robust extra-virgin olive oil

2 rabbits (6 to 8 pounds total), cut into serving pieces

fine sea salt and freshly ground black pepper

4 small carrots, peeled and thinly sliced

3 celery stalks, thinly sliced

1/2 medium onion, peeled and coarsely chopped

2 garlic cloves, peeled and sliced

large pinch of saffron

2 teaspoons hot *pimentón* pepper

8 cups water

2¹/2 cups (1 pound and 1¹/2 ounces) paella rice

1/2 pound fresh green beans, trimmed and cut into 1-inch pieces

1 spicy sausage, such as chorizo or linguiça, cut into 1/2-inch slices

I love paella and have made many versions, but one important characteristic always eluded me—the rice on the bottom never caramelized. I discovered why when I read an article in *Fine Cooking* magazine written by Norberto Jorge, who owns two restaurants that specialize in paella. The pan I was using wasn't large enough. He specifies an eighteen-inch pan for a paella to serve six to eight. In a pan this size, the rice layer is no more than 1/2 inch, so that a crispy bottom forms when all the liquid has evaporated.

My favorite way to cook this dish is in my wood-fired oven at our country house. Lacking such an oven, cook it on a preheated baking stone in a conventional oven (make sure the large pan will fit), or on top of the stove, spanning two burners, or on a grill over a hardwood charcoal fire.

A robust, Tuscan-style oil works with this recipe, but if you want to match the oil to the country of the recipe's origin, use a more delicate extra-virgin olive oil, such as an Arbequina.

The type of rice is important. Short-grained rice such as Bomba (see Resources) will soak up liquid at just the right rate. Paella is a dish that originated in Valencia and traditionally included rabbit, so this one does as well.

Plan your schedule so you can soak the beans overnight.

1. The evening before you plan to make the dish, put the beans in a bowl, add cold water to cover them by 3 inches, and leave them at room temperature overnight. The next day, drain them and set aside.

2. If you are baking the paella in a conventional oven, put a baking stone on the bottom shelf and preheat the oven to 400°F for 45 minutes.

3. Heat an 18-inch paella pan over two burners or on a grill with a medium-hot fire underneath. Add the extra-virgin olive oil and heat it until it trembles, becomes aromatic, and easily coats the bottom of the pan.

4. Season the rabbit pieces with salt and pepper and brown them in the olive oil, turning once. Remove the rabbit and set aside. Add the carrots, celery, onion, and garlic to the pan. Sprinkle with salt and a few grindings of black pepper and cook until the onions are translucent, 5 to 10 minutes.

5. Meanwhile heat a small skillet over high heat. When a drop of water dances on the surface, add the saffron and shake the pan until the threads become brittle, about 30 seconds. Turn off the heat and add a few tablespoons of water to the pan. Pour the saffron water into the vegetables and add the *pimentón*. Add the drained soaked beans, the water, and ½ teaspoon salt. Bring to a simmer. Continue cooking on the burners or grill (cover the grill if the fire has reduced to medium), or transfer to the oven.

6. Cook at a simmer until the beans are about halfway done and have absorbed about half of the liquid, 20 to 25 minutes.

7. Sprinkle the rice into the pan, return the rabbit pieces, and tuck the green beans and sausage slices into the rice. Don't stir after the rice has been added.

8. If cooking on a grill, check the fire. Add more charcoal if the fire is waning. When the liquid returns to a simmer, continue to cook until the rice is tender, all the liquid is absorbed, and the rice on the bottom crackles and smells toasty, another 20 to 25 minutes.

9. Remove from the heat, cover with a kitchen towel, and let the paella rest for 5 or 10 minutes. Serve directly from the pan if the size of your table permits.

TURKEY TONNATO

6 TO 8 SERVINGS

THE TURKEY:

2- to 2½-pound half turkey breast, skin and bones removed

fine sea salt

1½ cups (12 ounces) dry white wine

1½ cups (12 ounces) water, plus more if needed

½ a medium onion, peeled

1 carrot, peeled and thickly sliced

1 celery stalk, thickly sliced

1 bay leaf

6 whole peppercorns

THE SAUCE:

3 ounces tuna, either canned or poached in extra-virgin olive oil (see recipe, p. 115)

4 anchovy filets, either purchased or *crudo* packed in salt (see recipe, p. 123), rinsed and patted dry

½ cup (4 ounces) medium extra-virgin olive oil

1 teaspoon lemon juice

2 tablespoons salted capers, rinsed and patted dry

2 tablespoons chopped flat-leaf parsley

1 lemon, halved and cut into slices

This is a version of the classic vitello tonnato, an Italian dish made with poached veal in a tuna sauce, but I've substituted turkey breast for veal. It is good for parties or picnics and can be made ahead. In fact, it's better if it sits at least overnight to meld the flavors.

Many tonnato recipes include an egg yolk and heavy cream, but this one lets the taste of the olive oil shine and makes a lighter sauce.

If you're serving it as a lunch or dinner main course, add something colorful to the plate such as a radicchio or beet salad.

1. Put the turkey breast in a casserole that fits it snugly. Sprinkle it with fine sea salt. Add the wine and water. If the turkey is not submerged, add more water.

2. Bring to a boil. Skim any foam that rises to the top. Add the onion, carrot, celery, bay leaf, and peppercorns. Reduce the heat to a simmer and partially cover the pot. If the turkey persists in floating, cover it with a piece of parchment paper.

3. Cook at a simmer until the meat registers 160°F on an instant-read thermometer, about 1 hour.

4. Remove from the heat and let the turkey cool in the broth.

5. Put the tuna and anchovies in the bowl of a small processor. With the motor running, drizzle in the extra-virgin olive oil as if making mayonnaise. Remove the sauce from the processor. Whisk in the lemon juice. Whisk in ½ cup of the turkey poaching liquid until the sauce is the consistency of heavy cream. Add salt if necessary.

6. Slice the meat into ¼-inch slices across the grain. Attractively arrange the slices in a serving dish deep enough to accommodate the sauce. Spoon the sauce over the turkey.

7. Cover and refrigerate at least 4 hours before serving.

8. Remove the dish from the refrigerator 30 minutes before serving. Smooth the top with a spatula. Scatter the capers and chopped parsley on top and arrange the lemon slices around the edge of the dish.

COMMUNITY MILLING

In 2008, there were thirty-six mills processing olives for oil in California. Many of the mills' owners also grow olives or buy olives from specific growers year after year to sell under their own label. The mills also custom press fruit for growers who don't have mills, and many offer bottling, labeling, and, in some cases, storage services. Depending on their capacity, most millers set a minimum weight—often a thousand pounds, sometimes one ton—for a custom pressing of olives, or a minimum fee for quantities that don't meet the weight requirement.

This leaves the small producers, those with only a few dozen trees, in a quandary. How will they transform their precious crop into olive oil? Luckily for them, there are at least five mills throughout California—Dry Creek, McEvoy, the Olive Press, Figueroa, and Pasolivo—that offer community press days, events that allow people to pool their fruit with other small growers. The fruit is weighed, then after the olive oil is made

and the final quantity known, each contributor's share is calculated. At the community press day that I attended, one person contributed twelve pounds of olives and asked the inevitable question: "How much oil will I get?" A ballpark estimate determined about four ounces. At sixty cents a pound for milling, the contributor deemed it rather expensive. Such are the realities of extra-virgin olive oil.

Mills that offer community pressings give guidelines on their web sites including suggested limits (growers with more than three hundred pounds should team up with others to meet the minimum for a custom run), condition of the olives (stage of ripeness, cleanliness, picked within twenty-four hours, free of olive-fly infestation, and sometimes type of cultivars), and appropriate containers for transporting the olives (no paper or plastic bags).

During the community press day that I witnessed, olive growers came in waves, olive bins stacked in pickup trucks, smaller containers in hatchbacks or in the trunks of family sedans, and patiently waited in line at the weigh-in station. Some people were dressed in work clothes, others bejeweled as if stepping out for the evening. They lugged olives of every description—huge black Sevillanos, shriveled Koroneikis, Manzanillos swollen with water. They heeded the ban on plastic bags—I saw olives in galvanized wash tubs, hardware buckets, and purchased-for-the-occasion rope-handled blue plastic bins that still sported their price tags.

Many old-timers were nonchalant, hefting bins onto the scales in a businesslike manner. Others new to the game were visibly excited, snapping pictures while their olives were weighed and going inside to watch the operation. Some were solemn, as if handing over their first-born child (six people quietly ushered eight pounds to the scale).

The millers scrutinized every batch, as if trying to detect real coins from counterfeit, asked questions about suspect fruit, and reserved the right to refuse olives that they deemed unsound.

Some mills ask people to arrive with containers to take home the pressed olive oil, others store the finished oil for a few months in stainless-steel tanks covered with inert gas and remove the settled particulates from the bottom of the tanks before bottling the oil. Then, on a designated day, people return to claim their portion of liquid goodness.

DESSERTS

Simon Hopkinson muses in his book, *Roast Chicken and Other Stories*, "I wonder why it has taken us so long to become interested in using olive oil." I could say the same thing about baking with olive oil. After years of using butter almost exclusively, my discovery of olive oil was liberating. Now I'm always looking at dessert recipes in a new light, imagining their taste with extra-virgin olive oil instead of butter. I encourage you to look at some of your favorites the same way.

POUND CAKE WITH CANDIED ORANGE PEEL

extra-virgin olive oil for the pan

1½ cups (7½ ounces by weight) unbleached all-purpose flour

1 teaspoon baking powder

¼ teaspoon fine sea salt

6 tablespoons (3 ounces) extra-virgin olive oil or orange olive oil

1 cup (7 ounces by weight) granulated cane sugar

2 extra-large eggs at room temperature

½ teaspoon pure vanilla extract

⅓ cup (2⅔ ounces) buttermilk at room temperature

3 ounces candied orange peel, finely chopped

Although a pound cake is traditionally made with butter, this olive oil version is a worthy variation. Olive oil's monounsaturated fat has a small crystal that gives a fine texture to the cake. Butter, on the other hand, forms large fat crystals that trap large air pockets, which can rise in the batter as the cake bakes and escape, making the cake denser. Olive oil also contains tocopherols, antioxidants that slow the staling process, so cakes made with olive oil stay fresh longer.

It is always safe to use a delicate olive oil for baking so that the taste doesn't dominate. I have made this cake with a delicate extra-virgin olive oil, a medium extra-virgin olive oil, and an orange olive oil and liked them all.

Use high-quality orange peel or candy it yourself. Lacking good orange peel, substitute two teaspoons of grated orange zest. Add it after the sugar and olive oil have been mixed together, and use an orange or blood orange olive oil.

1. Preheat the oven to 350°F with the rack positioned in the middle. Oil an 8½-by-4½-inch loaf pan.

2. Sift the flour, baking powder, and salt together into a bowl. Set aside.

3. Beat the olive oil and sugar on medium speed in the bowl of a stand mixer with the paddle until well combined and slightly fluffy, scraping down the sides of the bowl a few times. (This mixture will not be as airy as a beaten butter-sugar mixture.)

4. Break the eggs into a small bowl and beat them lightly with a fork. With the mixer running, drizzle the eggs into the bowl a little at a time, waiting for each addition to become incorporated before adding more.

5. Stir the vanilla into the buttermilk.

6. Add the dry ingredients in three additions, alternating with the buttermilk (start and end with the dry ingredients).

7. Beat the orange peel into the batter until it is just combined.

8. Pour the batter into the baking pan and bake until puffed and browned and a skewer inserted in the center comes out clean, 45 to 55 minutes.

9. Cool the cake on a rack then remove it from the pan.

WALNUT-ROSEMARY BISCOTTI

2¼ cups (11¼ ounces by weight) unbleached all-purpose flour

1 teaspoon baking powder

1 teaspoon fine sea salt

¾ cup (5¼ ounces by weight) granulated cane sugar

1 extra-large egg

½ cup (4 ounces) buttermilk

¼ cup (2 ounces) robust extra-virgin olive oil

¾ cup (3⅓ ounces by weight) walnuts, lightly toasted and roughly chopped

1 tablespoon chopped fresh rosemary

I like to use herbs—such as rosemary—that are usually associated with savory dishes in desserts because they add a surprise taste twist.

The buttermilk tenderizes these cookies, putting them on the less-crunchy end of the biscotti spectrum.

The International Olive Council recommends a reduction of 25 percent when converting a recipe from butter to olive oil (use three-quarters of a cup or six ounces of oil instead of one cup of butter), but I think substituting half the amount of butter with oil works best in this recipe.

1. Preheat the oven to 350°F with the rack positioned in the middle. Line the bottom of a baking pan with parchment paper.

2. Sift the flour, baking powder, salt, and sugar together into a medium-sized bowl. Set aside.

3. In a small bowl, whisk the egg, buttermilk, and extra-virgin olive oil together.

4. Stir the wet ingredients into the dry ingredients with a large spoon until a shaggy mass forms.

5. Stir the walnuts and rosemary into the rough dough until they are evenly distributed.

6. Turn the dough out onto a lightly floured work surface. Knead it a few times to incorporate crumbs and make it smooth. Divide the dough in half. Roll each half into a log about 1¾ inches in diameter and 10 inches long.

7. Transfer the logs to the prepared baking pan. Lightly pat down the tops of the logs with your hand.

8. Bake, rotating the pan 180 degrees halfway through the cooking time, until the tops are lightly browned and a skewer inserted into the center of a log comes out clean, 20 to 25 minutes.

9. Let the logs cool on a wire rack.

10. Line the bottoms of two baking pans with parchment paper (you can reuse the parchment from the first baking). If you have turned off the oven, preheat it once again to 350°F and position a second rack.

11. Using a sharp knife, cut each log on the diagonal into ½-inch slices. Place the slices cut side up on the baking pans.

12. Bake, rotating the pans 180 degrees halfway through the cooking time, until the tops and bottoms are lightly browned, 10 to 15 minutes.

13. Let the cookies cool completely on wire racks. Store in an airtight container for up to 1 week.

EXTRA-VIRGIN OLIVE OIL ICE CREAM WITH VANILLA BEAN

1 QUART

1¼ cups (10 ounces) whole milk

⅔ cup (4⅔ ounces by weight) granulated cane sugar, divided

½ vanilla bean, split

3 extra-large egg yolks

1½ cups (12 ounces) heavy whipping cream

6 tablespoons (3 ounces) robust extra-virgin olive oil at refrigerator temperature

Pizzeria Pico in Larkspur, California, has a special machine that makes soft ice cream. The restaurant serves swirls of the ice cream with a generous topping of DaVero extra-virgin olive oil and a sprinkling of salt. It's a taste revelation. After sampling it, I began thinking about making ice cream with olive oil in it instead of on it and came up with this recipe. A robust extra-virgin olive oil replaces some of the egg yolks, lending its special flavor. If you want to accentuate the olive oil's savory notes, sprinkle a little fleur de sel or even a grinding of fresh black pepper over each serving.

The custard needs to be refrigerated overnight before churning, so make it a day ahead.

1. Stir the milk and ⅓ cup of the sugar together in a saucepan. Scrape the seeds from the vanilla bean into the pan and then add the bean. Bring the milk to a boil.

2. Remove the pan from the heat, cover the top of the pan with plastic wrap, and steep at room temperature for one hour.

3. Strain the milk through a sieve into a saucepan and bring it to a simmer.

4. While the milk is heating, in the bowl of a stand mixer fitted with the whisk attachment, beat the egg yolks and the remaining ⅓ cup sugar over medium speed until the mixture is pale and thick. Turn the machine to low speed and slowly pour the hot milk into the yolks and sugar.

5. Return the mixture to the saucepan and cook, stirring constantly, until the mixture thickens slightly and registers 160°F on an instant-read thermometer. Strain it into a bowl, stir in the cream, cover, and refrigerate overnight.

6. The next day, stir the olive oil into the custard and churn in an ice cream maker according to the manufacturer's instructions.

ALMOST FLOURLESS CHOCOLATE CAKE

7 ounces 70% dark chocolate, coarsely chopped

1/2 cup (4 ounces) either delicate or robust extra-virgin olive oil

1 cup (7 ounces by weight) granulated cane sugar, divided

5 extra-large eggs at room temperature, separated

2 tablespoons unbleached all-purpose flour

1/8 teaspoon fine sea salt

powdered sugar for dusting

whipped cream for serving (optional)

I have made this cake countless times with butter. It is easy to assemble and always garners raves from guests. Now I have a new way of making one of my favorites—using olive oil instead.

A delicate olive oil mimics the flavor profile of the butter version of this cake, although the oil adds an underlying taste. When made with a robust olive oil, the flavor is more pronounced—it is on equal footing with the chocolate rather than being a nuance.

Use a dark chocolate you like that has a cocoa content of 70 percent.

1. Preheat the oven to 350°F with the rack positioned in the middle.

2. Line the bottom of a 9-by-3-inch round cake pan with parchment paper.

3. Put the chocolate in a large stainless-steel bowl and melt it over simmering water. Whisk it until it is smooth.

4. Add the olive oil, whisking in a steady stream. Whisk in 2/3 cup of the sugar, the egg yolks, then the flour and salt.

5. Put the egg whites in the bowl of a stand mixer and beat on medium speed with the whisk attachment until they start to foam. Add about a third of the remaining 1/3 cup of sugar. Beat until the whites become opaque, then add another third of the sugar. When the whites begin to increase in volume and become firmer, add the rest of the sugar and turn the mixer speed to high. Beat until the whites form soft peaks when the whisk is lifted from the bowl. They will still look slightly wet.

6. Fold the whites into the chocolate mixture in two additions.

7. Pour the batter into the pan and bake until the cake is puffed and a skewer inserted into the center comes out clean or with only a few crumbs clinging to it, 35 to 40 minutes.

8. Let the cake cool completely, still in the pan, on a rack. It will deflate as it cools.

9. Run a table knife around the edge of the pan and invert the cake onto a serving plate. Peel off the parchment paper.

10. Lightly dust the top of the cake with powdered sugar. Serve at room temperature, with a dollop of whipped cream, if desired.

LEMON MADELEINES

1 cup (5 ounces by weight) unbleached all-purpose flour, plus more for the molds

1 teaspoon baking powder

3 extra-large eggs, at room temperature

pinch of fine sea salt

1 tablespoon mild honey

2/3 cup (4 1/2 ounces by weight) granulated cane sugar

zest of 1 lemon, preferably Meyer

6 tablespoons (3 ounces) Meyer lemon olive oil, plus more for the molds

1 tablespoon pure lemon extract

Proust would be astounded at the change in this recipe—an adaptation of a Gaston Lenôtre recipe that uses Meyer lemon olive oil instead of butter—but I'm sure this version will make you a convert.

The pans for madeleines are plates with depressions for each cookie. I prefer the metal ones with the larger indentations. If you have only one pan, refrigerate the extra batter while the first batch bakes. Unmold the cookies, rinse the indentations with hot water without using soap, dry carefully, then oil and flour them again before baking the second batch.

The batter sits in the refrigerator overnight, so start a day ahead.

1. Stir the flour and baking powder together and set aside.

2. Using the whisk attachment, start to beat the eggs, salt, and honey in the bowl of a stand mixer on medium speed. With the mixer running, gradually add the sugar. Turn the speed to high and beat until pale, thick, and double in volume, 3 to 4 minutes.

3. Remove the bowl from the mixer. Sift the flour mixture over the batter then fold it in with a spatula. Zest the lemon peel directly into the bowl, add the olive oil and lemon extract, and fold all into the batter.

4. Cover the bowl with plastic wrap and refrigerate overnight.

5. The next day, preheat the oven to 400°F with the rack positioned in the middle. Carefully oil the inside of the indentations on a madeleine pan. Use a sieve to dust each one with flour, then tap out the excess.

6. Gently stir the batter with a spatula to make sure that it is homogeneous. Fill each indentation about ¾ full. Bake, rotating the pans 180 degrees halfway through the baking time, until the cookies are puffed and lightly browned, 5 to 6 minutes. Remove from the oven and cool on a rack for about 5 minutes. You should be able to pick up the pan but the cookies will still be warm. Invert the pan and rap the edge on a counter to dislodge the cookies.

7. When the madeleines are completely cool, store them in an airtight container at room temperature. They will keep for about 4 days.

PAN CON CHOCOLATE

8 ounces 64% dark chocolate, coarsely chopped

2/3 cup (5 1/4 ounces) heavy whipping cream

1/3 cup (1 ounce by weight) powdered cane sugar

3 tablespoons (1 1/2 ounces) delicate extra-virgin olive oil

4 pieces of crusty bread

2 tablespoons orange or blood orange oil for drizzling

fleur de sel

This is my version of a dessert I couldn't resist at Laiola, a Catalan-inspired restaurant in San Francisco. At the restaurant, a plate held a scoop of ganache and a slice of rustic grilled bread. A delicate California Arbequina olive oil was drizzled over all. I mounded the ganache on the bread and took bites, the olive oil dripping from my fingers. It was delicious.

The restaurant used a mix of dark and milk chocolate, but I prefer all dark chocolate (Valrhona's fruity Manjari is a good choice). I've taken the liberty of using a delicate extra-virgin olive oil instead of butter to make the ganache.

An immersion blender ensures the proper emulsification of the ganache.

1. Put the chocolate in a 1-quart vessel, preferably a clear one designed for use with an immersion blender.

2. Put the cream and sugar in a small saucepan and bring to a boil over medium heat, whisking to dissolve the sugar.

3. Immediately pour the hot cream over the chocolate. Let it sit 1 minute. Blend the two together with an immersion blender using a stirring motion, going to the bottom of the vessel, until the ganache becomes less shiny and thickens to a puddinglike consistency, 1 to 2 minutes.

4. Add the olive oil in a steady stream, blending constantly. Pour the ganache into a bowl and let it cool to room temperature. Cover the bowl with plastic wrap without touching the ganache. Keep the ganache in a cool room until it sets, preferably overnight.

5. To serve, toast bread slices and put them on plates. Scoop balls of ganache and put them next to the toasts. Drizzle both the chocolate and the toast with orange olive oil and sprinkle with fleur de sel.

6. The ganache will keep in the refrigerator for at least a week. Bring it to room temperature before serving.

TRUFFLES WITH ORANGE OLIVE OIL

ABOUT 30 1-INCH TRUFFLES

Follow the directions for making ganache, but use orange or blood orange olive oil instead of delicate extra-virgin.

1. Let the ganache rest in the bowl in a cool room for at least 4 hours or overnight.

2. To roll the truffles, place a piece of parchment paper on a baking pan. Use a 1-inch ice cream scoop to make balls of ganache. Put them on the baking pan.

3. Put about ½ cup unsweetened natural cocoa powder in a medium bowl. Dust your palms with some of the cocoa powder. Briefly roll the truffles between your palms to smooth them, then drop them into the bowl of cocoa powder. After you have made 6 truffles, shake the bowl to completely cover them with cocoa powder. Transfer the truffles to a plate with cocoa powder-dusted fingers.

4. If you are not serving the truffles immediately, refrigerate them in a bowl with some cocoa powder so they won't stick together. Before serving, put them on a plate and let them come to room temperature. They will keep for at least a week in the refrigerator.

SEMOLINA CAKE WITH DRUNKEN GRAPES

¾ cup (6 ounces) Moscato

8 ounces seedless grapes (about 40), halved

⅓ vanilla bean

1½ cups (7½ ounces by weight) unbleached all-purpose flour

¾ cup (4½ ounces by weight) semolina flour

1¾ teaspoons baking powder

¼ teaspoon fine sea salt

4 extra-large eggs, at room temperature

1¾ cups (12¼ ounces by weight) granulated cane sugar, divided

1 teaspoon pure vanilla extract

⅔ cup (5¼ ounces) delicate extra-virgin olive oil with tropical notes

This recipe was inspired by a dessert I had at A Voce restaurant in Manhattan. Semolina flour, the finely ground endosperm of durum wheat, adds a rustic note to this cake and gives it a slight crunch. The olive oil gives it a light texture, the syrup makes it moist, and the grapes are a surprise addition.

Serve small glasses of the Moscato wine with the cake as a special treat.

1. Pour the wine into a small bowl. Add the grapes. Scrape the vanilla seeds into the bowl and add the bean as well. Macerate the grapes for 30 minutes. Lift them out with a slotted spoon and reserve the wine, vanilla seeds, and bean.

2. Preheat the oven to 350°F, positioning the rack in the middle. Line the bottom of a 9-by-3-inch round cake pan with parchment paper.

3. Sift both flours, baking powder, and salt into a bowl. Set aside.

4. Put the eggs in the bowl of a stand mixer. Beat with the paddle on medium speed, gradually adding 1½ cups of the sugar. Turn to medium-high speed and beat until well combined, about 2 minutes.

5. Turn the mixer speed to low. Add the vanilla extract. With the mixer running, gradually add the dry ingredients in 3 additions, alternating with the olive oil in 2 additions (start and end with the dry ingredients). Fold half of the macerated grapes into the batter with a spatula.

6. Pour the batter into the pan and bake until the top is golden brown and a skewer inserted into the center comes out clean, 40 to 45 minutes.

7. Let the cake cool completely, still in the pan, on a rack. Run a table knife around the edge of the pan and invert the cake onto a plate. Peel off the parchment paper and turn the cake right side up onto a serving platter.

8. Poke holes with a skewer at 1-inch intervals in top of the cake, stopping before reaching the bottom.

9. Make a sugar syrup by boiling the reserved wine mixture with the remaining ¼ cup sugar until it reduces by half. Strain the syrup.

10. Spoon the warm syrup over the cake. Serve with the reserved macerated grapes.

Resources

CALIFORNIA OLIVE OIL COUNCIL

888 718 9830

www.cooc.com

This site gives information about California olive oil production, lists members, and names oils that have achieved seal certification.

CORTI BROTHERS

800 509 3663

www.cortibros.biz

In addition to groceries, this special store in Sacramento, California, carries an array of extra-virgin olive oils, including a good selection from California, balsamic vinegar, and salt cod.

CUBE MARKETPLACE

888 237 2782

www.cubemarketplace.com

Here is an online source for Pondicherry peppercorns.

FORNO BRAVO COOKING

800 407 5119

www.fornobravo.com

Forno Bravo is an online source for type 00 flour.

GOUMANYAT & SON ROYAUME

33 01 44 78 96 74

www.goumanyat.com

This is a don't-miss stop if you are in Paris. It's a colorful shop that carries practically all of the spices needed for these recipes.

INTERNATIONAL OLIVE COUNCIL

www.internationaloliveoil.org

The Olive Oil Council's site provides information about the worldwide production of olives and olive oils.

KATZ AND COMPANY STORE

800 676 7176

www.katzandco.com

In addition to selling their own brand of olive oils, this store also carries other artisanal California extra-virgin olive oils.

LA TIENDA

800 710 4304

www.tienda.com

This is a source for paella pans, rice, capers in sea salt, saffron, *pimentón* paprika, and salt cod for *pil pil*.

LE SANCTUAIRE

315 Sutter St.

San Francisco, CA

415 986 4216

www.le-sanctuaire.com

This store is a favorite for local chefs to shop. The spice selection is carefully selected and is a good source for *za'atar*, ras el hanout, Aleppo pepper, and cubeb pepper.

LOS ANGELES INTERNATIONAL EXTRA-VIRGIN OLIVE OIL COMPETITION

www.laoliveoilcomp.com

Results of the competition and contact information for the medalists can be found on this web site.

MARKET HALL FOODS

888 952 4005

www.markethallfoods.com

Market Hall Foods has two retail locations in California, one in Oakland and the other in Berkeley. Both carry a good selection of extra-virgin olive oil, including many from California, vinegars, capers, and paella rice. They also accept online orders.

OLIVE OIL TASTING WHEEL

www.aromadictionary.com/
articles/oliveoil_article.html

This tasting wheel, developed by Australian olive oil expert Richard Gawel, offers an extensive listing of olive oil descriptors.

PENZEYS SPICES

800 741 7787

www.penzeys.com

Here is another source for Aleppo pepper, *za'atar*, and many other spices.

SUR LA TABLE

866 328 5412

www.surlatable.com

This source has heavy casseroles, skillets, saucepans, and other cookware available on the Internet, by catalog, or in their more than fifty retail stores in the United States.

THE OLIVE OIL SOURCE

805 688 1014

www.oliveoilsource.com

This site has extensive information about olive oil, supplies, and presses, as well as an online newsletter.

THE OLIVE PRESS

800 965 4839

www.theolivepress.com

The Olive Press sells their own extra-virgin olive oils and flavored oils, as well as other artisanal California extra-virgin olive oils, at two retail locations and online.

THE SPANISH TABLE

www.spanishtable.com

The Spanish Table has four retail locations. See their web site for phone numbers and online ordering. It's another source for paella pans, paella rice, *pimentón* paprika, saffron, and *cazuelas*.

THE SPICE HOUSE

www.thespicehouse.com

This spice emporium has five retail locations. See their web site for addresses or to order online.

UNIVERSITY OF CALIFORNIA DAVIS EXTENSION SERVICES

http://cesonoma.ucdavis.edu

This site includes a wealth of information about olive oil, as well as issues of *First Press*, the newsletter about olive oil production.

WE OLIVE

www.weolive.com

We Olive are franchise stores in various locations. See their web site for addresses. They carry a good selection of California extra-virgin olive oils.

WILLIAMS-SONOMA

877 812 6235

www.williams-sonoma.com

Williams-Sonoma sells heavy casseroles, skillets, saucepans, and other cookware online, through a catalog, or in their two hundred retail stores throughout the country.

YOLO COUNTY FAIR

www.yolocountyfair.net

This county fair in Northern California holds an olive oil competition that attracts many California olive oils.

Bibliography

Aidells, Bruce. *Bruce Aidells's Complete Book of Pork: A Guide to Buying, Storing, and Cooking the World's Favorite Meat*. New York: HarperCollins, 2004.

Aidells, Bruce, and Denis Kelly. *The Complete Meat Cookbook*. New York: Houghton Mifflin, 1998.

Armisen, Raymond, and André Martin. *Les Recettes de la Table Niçoise*. Strasbourg: Librairie Istra, 1972.

Ayer, Frederick. "The Sacramento Valley Olive Experience," *Edible Sacramento*, Winter 2007, pp. 33–34.

Boskou, Dimitrios, editor. *Olive Oil Chemistry and Technololgy*. Champaign, Illinois: AOCS Press, 2006.

Brancq, Isabel. *Cakes et Terrines*. Paris: Hachette Livre, 2002.

Bullard, Mary A. *Cumberland Island: A History*. Athens, GA: University of Georgia Press, 2003.

Cox, Jeff. "California Olive Oil, Entering a Golden Age." *The Art of Eating*, Fall 2006, pp. 11–19.

Dambeck, Steven. "The Essence of a Craftsman." *Edible Sacramento*, Winter 2005, pp. 22–23.

David, Elizabeth. *English Bread and Yeast Cookery*. New York: Viking Press, 1977.

Feibleman, Peter S., and the editors of Time-Life Books. *The Cooking of Spain and Portugal*. New York: Time-Life Books, 1969.

Field, Carol. *The Italian Baker*. New York: Harper & Row, 1985.

Gass, Gerald. *The Olive Harvest Cookbook*. San Francisco: Chronicle Books, 2004.

Greene, Alan. "Landmark Year for California Olive Ranch and Certified Olive Oils," *Olint*, October 2006, pp. 8–9.

Grigson, Jane. *The Art of Making Sausages, Pâtés, and Other Charcuterie*. New York: Alfred A. Knopf, 1980.

Gunstone, Frank D. *Rapeseed and Canola Oil: Production, Processing, Properties and Uses*. Oxford, UK: Blackwell Publishing, Ltd., 2004.

Harlow, Jay. *West Coast Seafood*. Seattle: Sasquatch Books, 1999.

Hinault, Francis, and Joseph Koscher. *Les Recettes de la Table Bretonne*. Paris: Editions Casteilla, 1986.

Hirigoyen, Gerald. *The Basque Kitchen*. New York: HarperCollins, 1999.

Historical Resource Evaluation Report. Berkeley Olive Association Historic District, Butte County, California. 03-BUT-70/149/99, P.M. 20.5/0.0-4.6/21.8 03207-382200, 382210, 382220

Hopkinson, Simon, with Lindsey Bareham. *Roast Chicken and Other Stories*. New York: Hyperion, 2006.

International Olive Council Sensory Analysis of Olive Oil. COI/T.20 Doc. No 15/REV2/ September, 2007.

Jenkins, Nancy Harmon. *The Essential Mediterranean: How Regional Cooks Transform Key Ingredients Into the World's Favorite Cuisines*. New York: HarperCollins, 2003.

Johnson, Paul. *Fish Forever: The Definitive Guide to Understanding, Selecting, and Preparing Healthy, Delicious, and Environmentally Sustainable Seafood*. New York: Wiley, 2000.

Jorge, Norberto. "Paella, Rice at Its Best."*Fine Cooking*, July 1999, no. 33, pp. 46–51.

Kiritsakis, Apostolos K. *Olive Oil: From the Tree to the Table*. Trumbull, Connecticut: Food & Nutrition Press, Inc., 1998.

Klein, Maggie Blyth. *The Feast of the Olive: Cooking with Olives and Olive Oil*. San Francisco: Chronicle Books, 1994.

Knickerbocker, Peggy. *Olive Oil: From Tree to Table*. San Francisco: Chronicle Books, 1997.

Koscher, Joseph, Antoine Diss, Francis Hinault, and Charles Euler. *Les Recettes de la Table Alsacienne*. Strasbourg: Librairie Istra, 1969.

Krasner, Deborah. *The Flavors of Olive Oil: A Tasting Guide and Cookbook*. New York: Simon & Schuster, 2002.

Leonard, Jonathan Norton, and the editors of Time-Life Books. *Latin American Cooking*. New York: Time-Life Books, 1968.

Marques, Xavier. "Corto Olive Company: Interview with Dino Cortopassi," *Olint*, October 2006, pp. 4–7.

Médecin, Jacques. *Cuisine Niçoise*. Middlesex, England: Penguin Books, 1983.

McGee, Harold. *On Food and Cooking: The Science and Lore of the Kitchen*. New York: Scribner, 2004.

Mitchell, John, historian, Cumberland Island National Seashore. Telephone conversation, April 2008.

Mueller, Tom. "Slippery Business: The Trade in Adulterated Olive Oil." *The New Yorker*, August 13, 2007, pp. 38–45.

Nickles, Harry G., and the editors of Time-Life Books. *Middle Eastern Cooking*. New York: Time-Life Books, 1969.

Reinhart, Peter. *American Pie: My Search for the Perfect Pizza*. Berkeley, CA: Ten Speed Press, 2003.

Rodgers, Judy. *The Zuni Cafe Cookbook: A Compendium of Recipes and Cooking Lessons from San Francisco's Beloved Restaurant*. New York: W. W. Norton, 2002.

Rodgers, Rick, editor. *The Baker's Dozen Cookbook: Become a Better Baker with 135 Foolproof Recipes and Tried-and-True Techniques*. New York: William Morrow, 2001.

Root, Waverley. *The Food of France*. New York: Alfred A. Knopf, 1958.

Rosenblum, Mort. *Olives: The Life and Lore of a Noble Fruit*. New York: North Point Press, 1996.

Sibbett, G. Steven, and Louise Ferguson. *Olive Production Manual*. Second Edition. Oakland, CA: University of California, 2005.

Simopoulos, Artemis P., and Francesco Visioli, editors. *More on Mediterranean Diets. World Review of Nutrition and Dietetics, Vol. 97*. Basel, Switzerland: Karger, 2007.

Taylor, Judith M. *The Olive in California: History of an Immigrant Tree*. Berkeley, CA: Ten Speed Press, 2000.

Trabocchi, Fabio. *Cucina of Le Marche*. New York: Ecco, Harper Collins, 2006.

Vergé, Roger. *Ma Cuisine du Soleil*. Paris: Editions Robert Laffont, 1978.

Vossen, Paul. "Tree Spacing for Super-High-Density Plantings," *Olint*, October 2006, pp. 20–22.

Vossen, Paul. "Olive Oil Yield," *First Press*, Fall 2006, pp. 1–3.

Vossen, Paul. "Progress on the USDA Standards for Olive Oil," *First Press*, Fall 2006, p. 3.

Wolfert, Paula. *Mediterranean Cooking*. New York: Ecco-Harper Collins, 1995.

Wright, Clifford A. *A Mediterranean Feast: The Story of the Birth of the Celebrated Cuisines of the Mediterranean from the Merchants of Venice to the Barbary Corsairs, with More than 500 Recipes*. New York: William Morrow and Company, Inc., 1999.

Acknowledgments

While working on this book, I was inspired and aided by many people and would like to thank them here.

John Mitchell for shedding light on the olive trees of Cumberland Island.

Dick Neilson for arranging a tour of McEvoy Ranch.

Darrell Corti for his suggestions and encouragement.

Patty Darragh for introductions to producers, providing olive oil samples, and supporting the taste panel.

Martha Casselman for editing this book's proposal under less than ideal conditions.

Jeanne Baumgarten for asking my advice about choosing olive oil.

My fellow olive oil slurpers on the taste panels for helping me learn more about olive oil.

Alexandra Kicenik Davarenne for helping me think about olive oil and food pairings.

Paul Vossen for his knowledge and insight and for offering the sensory evaluation course that put me on the olive oil path.

All the people in the profiles, who gladly shared their orchards, mills, and nurseries and generously gave me olive oils to sample.

The organizers of the Los Angeles Competition and the Yolo County Fair for inviting me to judge olive oil.

Dan Dodt for unraveling the intricacies of anchovy preparation.

Michèle Morainvillers, Gregory Johnson, Jennifer and Les Seely, and Linda Blacketer for tasting versions of the recipes.

Carole Bidnick, my agent, for believing in this book from the start.

Leslie Stoker, Luisa Weiss, Claire Bamundo, and the staff at Stewart, Tabori & Chang for making this book a reality.

Maren Caruso—assisted by Stacy Ventura, Jessica Beisler, Katie Christ, Christine Wolheim, and Rachel Leising—for providing beautiful photographs; LeAnna Weller Smith for a sensitive book design; and Ana DeBoo for careful copyediting.

And—most of all—Sidney, who not only read every word but waited patiently during countless dinner preparations while I rummaged through my collection of olive oils looking for just the right one to accompany a dish we were preparing.

Index (Page references in *italic* refer to illustrations.)

Conversion Chart

Weight Equivalents

The metric weights given in this chart are not exact equivalents, but have been rounded up or down slightly to make measuring easier.

AVOIRDUPOIS	METRIC
1/4 oz	7 g
1/2 oz	15 g
1 oz	30 g
2 oz	60 g
3 oz	90 g
4 oz	115 g
5 oz	150 g
6 oz	175 g
7 oz	200 g
8 oz (1/2 lb)	225 g
9 oz	250 g
10 oz	300 g
11 oz	325 g
12 oz	350 g
13 oz	375 g
14 oz	400 g
15 oz	425 g
16 oz (1 lb)	450 g
1 1/2 lb	750 g
2 lb	900 g
2 1/4 lb	1 kg
3 lb	1.4 kg
4 lb	1.8 kg

Volume Equivalents

These are not exact equivalents for American cups and spoons, but have been rounded up or down slightly to make measuring easier.

AMERICAN	METRIC	IMPERIAL
1/4 tsp	1.2 ml	
1/2 tsp	2.5 ml	
1 tsp	5.0 ml	
1/2 Tbsp (1.5 tsp)	7.5 ml	
1 Tbsp (3 tsp)	15 ml	
1/4 cup (4 Tbsp)	60 ml	2 fl oz
1/3 cup (5 Tbsp)	75 ml	2.5 fl oz
1/2 cup (8 Tbsp)	125 ml	4 fl oz
2/3 cup (10 Tbsp)	150 ml	5 fl oz
3/4 cup (12 Tbsp)	175 ml	6 fl oz
1 cup (16 Tbsp)	250 ml	8 fl oz
1 1/4 cups	300 ml	10 fl oz (1/2 pint)
1 1/2 cups	350 ml	12 fl oz
2 cups (1 pint)	500 ml	16 fl oz
2 1/2 cups	625 ml	20 fl oz (1 pint)
1 quart	1 liter	32 fl oz

Oven Temperature Equivalents

OVEN MARK	F	C	GAS
Very cool	250–275	130–140	1/2–1
Cool	300	150	2
Warm	325	170	3
Moderate	350	180	4
Moderately hot	375	190	5
	400	200	6
Hot	425	220	7
	450	230	8
Very hot	475	250	9